Golfing

On the World's
Most
Exceptional
Courses

MARK ROWLINSON

Golfing

On the World's
Most
Exceptional
Courses

Abbeville Press Publishers
New York   London

First published in the United States of America in
2005 by Abbeville Press, 137 Varick Street, New York,
NY 10013

First published in Great Britain in 2005 by Conran
Octopus Limited, a part of Octopus Publishing
Group, 2–4 Heron Quays, London E14 4JP

Text copyright © 2005 Mark Rowlinson
Book design and layout copyright
© 2005 Conran Octopus Limited

Library of Congress Cataloging-in-Publication Data

Rowlinson, Mark, 1948–
  Golfing on the world's most exceptional courses /
  Mark Rowlinson.—1st ed.
       p. cm.
1. Golf courses—Directories. 2. Golf resorts—
Directories. I. Title.
  GV975.R69 2005
  796.352'068'025—dc22
                            2005009741

First Edition
10 9 8 7 6 5 4 3 2 1

ISBN 0-7892-0866-0

Publishing Director: Lorraine Dickey
Commissioned by: Katey Day
Editor: Sybella Marlow
Art Director: Jonathan Christie
Designer: Victoria Burley
Illustrator: Russell Bell
Picture Research Manager: Liz Boyd
Picture Researcher: Sarah Hopper
Production Manager: Angela Couchman

Front jacket photograph: Courtesy of Fairmont Hotel
and Resorts, Alberta
Back jacket photograph: Tony Roberts/Corbis.
Printed in China

For bulk and premium sales and for text adoption
procedures, write to Customer Service Manager,
Abbeville Press, 137 Varick Street, New York, NY
10013 or call 1-800-ARTBOOK.

Contents

Introduction

It is January in England. Outside it is dark and dismal. And raining, of course. The fairways of the local golf courses are waterlogged. There are temporary greens and rubber mat tees. One can only dream of golf. And that is exactly what I have been doing in compiling this book, writing about some of the very best and most beautiful golf courses on earth.

There are around 32,000 golf courses throughout the world. So what were the criteria for selecting the 25 golf destinations in this book? First and foremost is the quality of the golf on offer. There is no point in travelling thousands of miles to play an average or mediocre golf course. If the destination was a resort, then it has to be special, offering service and accommodation on a par with its golf. And there has to be plenty of non-golfing activities, sporting and otherwise, to entertain those who do not want to golf. The surroundings have to be beautiful and uplifting. In a few cases — southwest Ireland, the Lancashire coast, and the Surrey heathlands, southwest of London — I have chosen a region studded with top-rate golf courses which are not in themselves resorts. In these cases I have selected an appropriate hotel or resort at which to stay, close to all the courses selected. I have been glad to consult widely with good golfers who play these courses and stay at these resorts, and their opinions have been a major factor in the selection process. So, too, has been the valuable experience of the professionals, the people who run golf travel and tourism companies, and in particular Ben Cowan-Dewar of GOLFTI.com, whose knowledge and wisdom has been indispensable.

The golf courses have been described from the point of view of a good player who is competent to play from the back tees. All distances are given in yards, as these are still used in North America and Great Britain. To convert to metres, multiply by 0.9144 or, more roughly, take off 10 per cent. I have not listed every facility at every resort, and this is particularly true of the golf facilities. It is safe to assume that they all offer golf club rental, professional lessons and good practice facilities. Cart rental is possible at many courses, but not all — especially some of the more traditional clubs in the British Isles, which actively encourage walking and ban the use of carts. All have well-stocked golf shops for the purchase of clubs, balls, clothing, golfing accessories, and souvenirs. Caddies are available at many courses, but they should be booked well in advance to avoid last minute disappointment. Handicap restrictions may apply on some courses, and at many of those in the British Isles visitors may be required to present a letter of introduction from their home club.

As these details change from time to time, it is essential to check the club or resort's website. Green fees can vary with the season or time of day, and some courses and resorts offer golf packages which will also be shown on the website. Demand to play on major championship courses, such as Pebble Beach or the Old Course, St. Andrews, is immense, and it is necessary to book long in advance.

Every effort has been made to check and re-check the facts contained in this book. The publishers will be grateful for any corrections or other information that will assist them in updating future editions.

OPPOSITE: THE 8TH GREEN AT PEBBLE BEACH, AND BEYOND IT STRETCHING INTO THE DISTANCE, THE 9TH AND 10TH FAIRWAYS — ONE OF THE GREATEST STRETCHES OF SEASIDE GOLF ON EARTH.

Hope Island Resort,
Queensland, Australia

Some of the most exciting new golf courses are springing up in Australia. Tom Doak's Barnbougle Dunes in Tasmania, the National Golf Club's Ocean and Moonah Courses in Victoria, and Kerry Packer's private family course at Ellerston in the Hunter Valley have immediately entered the upper echelons of Australian golf, right up there with traditional favourites Royal Melbourne, New South Wales, and Kingston Heath. That said, there are also some very routine new courses, built to a formula and totally uninteresting. Unfortunately, too many of Australia's resort courses are of this kind. One of the most notable exceptions is Hope Island, though its beginnings were unpromising.

OPPOSITE: STRETCHING TO 253 YARDS FROM THE BACK TEES, HOPE ISLAND'S 17TH IS A FORMIDABLE PAR 3.

A Japanese man, Mr. Isutani, had bought a dairy farm on Queensland's Gold Coast. It was flat and featureless. He wanted to build a golf course there and it had to be a good one. When he approached the design team of Peter Thomson, Michael Wolveridge, and Ross Perrett he explained that he had a generous budget and suggested they repeat the success they had had at Twin Waters (also on the Queensland Coast), where they had managed to build something akin to a British links course in an alien climate. "We jumped at the chance to do another manufactured links," said Wolveridge.

Peter Thomson won a total of five Open Championships. He did so because he understood fully the philosophy of playing links courses and had the technique and composure to execute finesse shots under extreme pressure. Playing in an era of un-watered fairways and hand-watered (if that) greens, he was a master of the ground game, running the approach shot along the fairway, between guardian bunkers and up and onto a firm green which could never have accepted the high-flown approach of today. When given the opportunity, Thomson likes nothing better than to design courses

that embrace those same testing challenges, so rarely seen today in this era of target golf.

Before they could start building the course they had to raise the whole site by 2 metres (6 feet) to protect it from flooding. They excavated over a million cubic metres of clay, leaving a lake 18 metres (60 feet) deep beside what is now the 18th hole, and covered the clay with a layer of sand to ensure good drainage. Because the whole thing was entirely artificial, Thomson and his team were given a free hand in shaping the ground. What they created was in the style of the seaside links on which Thomson had been so successful as a player. So the fairways are full of ridges, humps, bumps and swales, and traditional pot-bunkers. These are not merely cosmetic features off to the side of the fairway but are right in the middle of the fairways, rather like the Old Course at St. Andrews, requiring the player to think carefully on every shot. Because of the good drainage the fairways are fast running, encouraging the golfer to use the bump-and-run approach to many greens, most of which are raised in the style of the old-fashioned links courses.

THE APPROACH TO THE 9TH GREEN IS PLAYED TOWARDS THE IMPRESSIVE CLUBHOUSE.

The 1st green is typical, raised up to a metre (three feet) above the fairway. Here the approach that does not hold the putting surface will very likely roll off down one of the shaved banks into a hollow, from which the best play may well be with a judiciously weighted putter. It is the only bunkerless hole. A lake and two handsome fig trees dictate play on the first-rate 2nd, a par 5 which curves to the left along the lake and around the figs. These trees and a crescent-shaped bunker constrict the fairway at the range of a long drive, and for most golfers this is a genuine three-shot hole.

Deep bunkers are a threat on the 3rd, the first of the par 3s, demanding a full 200-yard carry from the back tee. The next short hole, the 5th, is only 154 yards long, but the green is small and deceptively angled from left to right behind a snaking bunker, and the tee shot must be very carefully judged.

Peter Thomson's 1955 Open Championship victory was at St. Andrews. He alludes to this on the 8th at Hope Island, calling the hole "Principal's Nose", after the bunkers which are such a threat to driving on the 16th on the Old Course. At Hope Island

there are a pair of bunkers on the right in the driving zone, and bunkers abound throughout the length of this par 5, as they do on the par-4 9th which conveniently returns to the clubhouse.

There are 120 pot-bunkers at Hope Island. Sometimes a single one is enough to affect play, such as the one guarding the 10th green. They litter the 11th and 12th fairways and will usually cost the golfer at least one shot, for they are deep, steeply-faced pits from which a long shot is nigh on impossible. On the 13th, five bunkers lurk in the driving zone, but it is

a long par 4, laying up short is not an option, particularly as the second shot must carry a stretch of water in the angle of the dog-leg to find the green. Both short holes on the back nine involve a carry over water, and from the back tees they are both substantial. The 14th measures 211 yards and the 17th a whopping 253 yards. Of course there are forward tees at more manageable distances, and for those uncertain of their skill there is a bail out area off to the right, from where the pitch is reasonably straightforward and there might just be a chance of single-putting for par.

THE FORMIDABLE CARRY ACROSS WATER ENCOUNTERED ON THE 13TH.

Hope Island keeps one of its best holes for last, a 565-yard par 5 with the lake for company all the way down the left-hand side. For the big-hitter hoping to get on in two there are three bunkers set into a ridge in driving range, forcing the tee shot towards the lake. Further bunkers thwart corner-cutting as the fairway gradually bears left around the lake, and the green is designed to repel weak approaches. It is not an easy hole to attack, nor is it particularly easy to play conservatively. A fine end to a good and challenging course.

Accommodation at Hope Island Resort itself is in villas, apartments, and luxury homes, and stay-and-play packages

THE DIFFICULTIES OF THE TEE-SHOT ON THE 2ND ARE CLEARLY APPARENT.

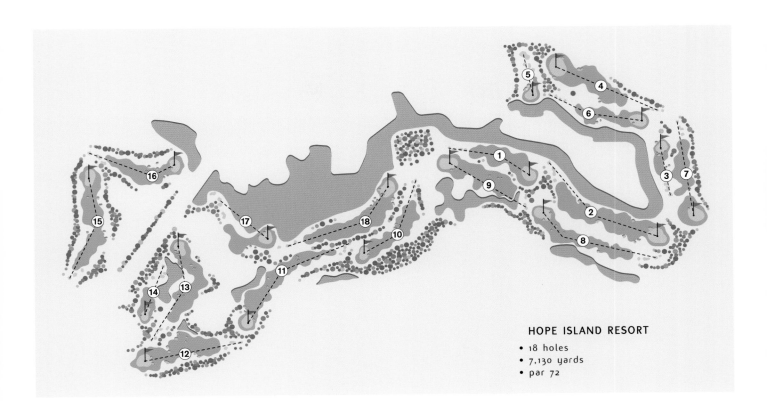

HOPE ISLAND RESORT

- 18 holes
- 7,130 yards
- par 72

offering golf and breakfast are available. Queensland's Gold Coast is brimming with bars and restaurants, and the Boardwalk Tavern at Hope Island's marina features a wine emporium and eleven beers on tap. Pat Cash, the five-times Grand Slam winner, has opened a tennis academy at the resort.

Only five minutes away is the Hyatt Regency Sanctuary Cove, a five-star, 247-bedroom resort based around a 1940s-style colonial lodge. Although it has all the latest electronic gadgetry to satisfy the most demanding business traveller, there is a relaxed pace to life here, not least in selecting wine: diners go down into the oak cellar themselves to choose their bottle from a vast range of Australia's finest. Here, too, there are first-rate tennis facilities and a very well equipped fitness centre. Sanctuary Cove's two golf courses are available for the use of guests, and surfing, scuba diving, swimming, hot-air ballooning, kart racing, and parasailing are among the more energetic activities on offer. This part of the Queensland coast is also a nature paradise, and trips to the Great Barrier Reef and the rainforest are but two of the "must sees". And of course Queensland's enviable sunny climate means that a visit at any time of year is delightful.

Golf in and around Hope Island Resort

Hope Island Resort
Hope Island Road
Hope Island
Queensland
Australia
Tel: +61 7 5530 9000
Email: *via website*
www.hir.com.au/contact.asp
www.hir.com.au/home.asp

Hyatt Regency Sanctuary Cove
Manor Circle
Sanctuary Cove
Queensland 4212
Australia
Tel: +61 7 5530 1234
Email: sanctuary@hyatt.co.au
http://sanctuarycove.regency.hyatt.com

The Empire Hotel and Country Club, Brunei

Lying only 400 km (250 miles) north of the Equator, Brunei is a small Islamic sultanate on the north coast of Borneo, known in the western world principally for its oil and gas wealth. It would be very wrong, nevertheless, to picture Brunei as a desolate spot with oil rigs belching forth flames and smoke, polluting the atmosphere and filtering out the sun's rays. In fact more than half of Brunei's land area is made up of unspoiled tropical rainforest, a naturalist's dream. Brunei is an old country, too, mentioned by Chinese writers as long ago as the 6th and 7th centuries. The present Sultan is the 29th in a reigning line stretching back over 600 years.

A FUSION OF EASTERN AND WESTERN ARCHITECTURE
GIVES THE EMPIRE HOTEL ITS DISTINCTIVE STYLE.

Looking out over the South China Sea, the Empire is Brunei's only beachside resort. To describe it as grand is a considerable understatement. It is vast (with 360 guest rooms in addition to 63 suites and enormous villas), opulent (the presidential suite has its own indoor swimming pool and private cinema), extensive (occupying 180 hectares or 445 acres), and successful (it has won a number of prestigious awards).

It would be perfectly possible to visit the Empire for a week or two, never leave its grounds and be entirely satisfied, but it would be a pity to miss out on the varied and very different experiences offered by the Brunei-Muara district in which the resort is located that you might not otherwise have a chance to experience. For instance, the capital's water village, Kampung Ayer, is built on stilts rambling over the Brunei River. Much the best way to see it is to take a water taxi through the maze of waterways, disembarking from time to time to see the markets and stalls selling exotic fish, meats, vegetables, flowers, and fruits. And Kampung is much more than a market, for also suspended above the water are homes, mosques, and all the usual buildings of urban life, such as schools and hospitals. Another good market, Tamu Kianngeh on the banks of the Kianngeh River, sells local handicrafts as well as foodstuffs and medicinal herbs.

Because it is an Islamic sultanate, both the royal family and its religion are of fundamental importance to Brunei. The Sultan's palace is said to be the largest residential palace in the world. It is not open to the public, but a great deal of the exterior can be seen from the neighbouring Periaran Damuan Park, and at night its domes and minarets make a stunning background to dinner at one of the many open-air restaurants in the park. In the very heart of the city stands the imposing Sultan Omar Ali Salfuddien Mosque, an extraordinary creation of marble, gold, and glass reflected in a mirror-like expanse of water. Nearby are the Royal Regalia Building, the Lapau, the hall in which royal ceremonies are held, and the Dewan Majis, the parliament building. Yet only a 15-minute walk from here is Tasek Lama Park, a nature reserve and slice of genuine rainforest within the city's boundaries, complete with adventure trails and jogging and walking routes for those with sufficient energy.

ROCKY OUTCROPS ARE AN OCCASIONAL THREAT TO A WAYWARD SHOT DURING THE ROUND.

Naturally alcohol is not sold in Brunei. However, all is not lost for the parched golfer, as the Empire resort is a mere 20-minute drive from the Malaysian border, where alcohol is available, and in large quantities! The reputation of Malaysian liquor stores runs high, and they all carry a good selection of international beers, wines, and spirits. The Empire hotel does not charge corkage, moreover, and of course there is no mark-up, so guests are free to consume whatever they wish with their food at very much less than normal hotel prices. The food at the Empire is plentiful and distinctive, with the Spaghettini Restaurant specializing in Italian dishes and the beachside Pantal in a wide range of seafood. Chinese cuisine is featured in Li Gong, while the Atrium Café and Lobby Lounge offer lighter fare. The Spike Lounge and Bunker Café are to be found beside the golf course. For evening entertainment there is an art gallery, as well as a theatre, cinema, 10-pin bowling rink, and spa.

For non-golfing partners and those competent to do so, it is possible to play a chukka at the Sultan's own polo club, and there are leisure rides and treks in the Trijaya Jerudong Equestrian Park. Tennis, squash, and badminton are complemented by jet skiing and white-water rafting and those who want to shed a few pounds in a humid atmosphere need not bother to visit the sauna, as a mountain-bike race into the jungle will do the same job more than adequately!

It is quite common in the Far East to have floodlights installed on a golf course. Enthusiasm for the game is immense, and all the daylight hours as well as quite a few nocturnal ones are filled with players, especially on public-access courses. So close to the Equator, the sun sets swiftly and there is little or no twilight, and it would be terribly disappointing to play the 16th in daylight and then not to be able to complete the 17th as night had fallen. At the Empire, twilight and 9-hole floodlit green fees are available for hotel guests and walk-in visitors alike, and there is a special Wednesday deal of 9 holes of floodlit golf followed by a giant barbecue. Golfers unused to playing by floodlight will find that their distance perception is sometimes confused and reading tricky putting surfaces can be difficult, but the experience more than makes up for these minor quibbles.

For the most part, resort golf courses require their design teams to perform miracles. The course must be entirely playable by the occasional golfer or high handicapper who has paid the same green fee as the scratch player. He or she does not want to spend hours looking for lost golf balls, or freezing on the tee at the prospect of a compulsory carry over some ball-swallowing obstacle such as a jungle-filled ravine or alligator-infested lake! On the other hand, they may relish the choice between attempting the nearly impossible and taking a more sensible alternative route, probably at the cost of a stroke. Scratch players, on the other

NOT ONLY IS THE 15TH A HANDSOME HOLE, IT IS ALSO DEMANDING.

hand, take delight in being set difficult challenges and overcoming them. They need to be given risk — and subsequent reward if they execute the shot perfectly. Jack Nicklaus and his team seem to have got this complex formula just right on their 7,031-yard course at the Empire Country Club.

Essentially, the front 9 holes run over high ground, giving many fine seascapes and some interestingly shaped holes, while the back 9 makes an excursion down to the shores of the South China Sea before climbing to a climax on high ground once more. The start is gentle — an opportunity to lay the foundation for a good score — but all can be quickly lost on the par-3 4th with its tee shot all-carry over the corner of a pond. Position off the tee is all important on the 5th, a 407-yard par 4, played to a sloping fairway. If the tee shot can be held on the right of the fairway there follows a lovely approach shot to a well-bunkered green on high ground, offering a glorious view over the sea. However, if the tee shot drifts left there is little chance of hitting and holding this elusive green. It is followed by an excellent short two-shotter, only 357 yards from the very back, with a testing drive over a ravine to a narrow fairway, bunkered on the left and with cliffs falling away on the right.

In an effort to avoid the cliffs beside the green, many an approach shot is pulled up short into the expansive green-front bunker. Another cliff-side hole comes next, the 235-yard par-3 7th. It may have no bunkers and it plays downhill, but most tee-shots falling short bound off down to the right, lost for good. It is an all-or-nothing hole.

On the back 9 there is more emphasis on length, although the 440-yard par-4 11th plays downhill, making it seem somewhat shorter. The green is handsomely set above a lake. A stream cuts across the fairway just before the green on the slightly longer 13th, while

THE EMPIRE GOLF COURSE

- 18 holes
- 7,031 yards
- par 71

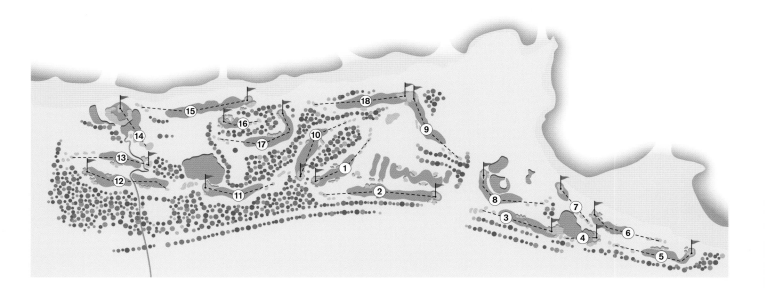

the 221-yard 14th is played across water to a distant green almost entirely surrounded by sand. Back beside the sea and running along the side of the shore, the 15th is a 549-yard par 5 on which almost any casual shot will find sand, and with the green angled round to the left beside the beach it is one of the most memorable holes on the course. The short 16th offers some respite before a testing pair of finishing holes. Accurate driving is essential on the 17th, with the need for a precisely placed tee-shot if there is to be a realistic chance of finding the hill-top green. At 476 yards, the 18th is right at the upper limit of par 4, and cliffs on the left threaten the wayward drive, although they grant the golfer superb views. Straightness is again required with the long approach shot, played to a green shared with the 9th, narrow and well-bunkered.

Contact:

The Empire Hotel and Country Club
Jerudong BG3122
Brunei Darussalam
Tel: +673 241 8888
E-mail: sales@theempirehotel.com
www.theempirehotel.com

Fairmont Banff Springs, Canada

The Banff Springs Hotel is one of the most imposing in the world, conceived on a scale that would be overwhelming in any setting other than the towering Rockies that surround it. Like a number of other famous resort hotels it was built by a railway company, in this case the Canadian Pacific Railway in 1888. In 1911 a 9-hole golf course was added for the amusement of guests, and this was expanded to 18 holes by a workforce of German prisoners during the First World War. In 1927 Stanley Thompson was commissioned to redesign the course. Looking back from a 21st-century viewpoint, it is easy to see that Thompson was without doubt the most distinguished Canadian architect of the last century, and one of the giants of the inter-war years in world terms. In addition to Banff Springs, Capilano in British Columbia, Jasper Park in Alberta, Highlands Links in Nova Scotia, and St. George's in Toronto are top-notch courses by any reckoning.

At Banff Springs, Thompson was given a magnificent canvas on which to work. Two mountain rivers, the Bow and the Spray, meet below the precipice on which the hotel stands, their waters clear blue under summer skies. Woods are abundant here, and Thompson was able to use the tall conifers to frame each hole without overwhelming it, to help the eye make the transition between the relatively level fairways and the lofty mountains beyond. Above all, Thompson was a master of bunkering. This is not to imply that he put in so many bunkers willy-nilly that every single imperfect shot ends up in sand, although there are close to 150 bunkers in his layout. His skill lay rather in using bunkers to affect the appearance of a hole; to deceive the eye in the judgement of distance; to make slopes and mounds appear different from what they are in reality; and to create a sense of scale in proportion to the mountains beyond each hole. The bunkering, then, has a ruggedness that is in keeping with the surroundings, and is not dwarfed into inadequacy by the sheer height of the mountains. In other words, one cannot help but notice the individual features of the course, despite the dramatic environment.

The course has never been tested by fields of high-quality professionals under tournament conditions, as it is too far from any major centre of population. Besides, this is a holiday resort with a short summer season. Guests do not want to have one of the hotel's major attractions denied them for the conflicting interests of a professional tour, which most of the time plays on courses that are not even half as good as Banff. But professionals have visited and played the course out of interest, and invariably they have gone away singing its praises. In 1992, golf course architect Bill Robinson was called in to add 9 further holes. He left Thompson's classic untouched, but when a new clubhouse was built to serve both courses it was located in a different position, and play on Thompson's course now starts on what was the old 5th hole. That might not seem particularly important, but it has given the course a different rhythm. It used to begin with a stunning tee-shot played across the Spray River to a distant fairway. That hole is now the 15th, by which time the golfer is in full flow and the carry over the river is rather less intimidating than it was on an opening hole. The most thrilling hole of all was the short 8th. There was a sense of build up to this climax to the outward 9. Now this comes as the 4th, and while there is no diminution in the quality of the golf thereafter, there is a slight sense of anticlimax that this particular excitement is over so early in the game.

THE DEVIL'S CAULDRON IS ONE OF THE WORLD'S GREAT SHORT HOLES, AND IT WOULD BE GREAT EVEN WITHOUT ITS MAGNIFICENT SETTING.

THE NEW CLUBHOUSE AT BANFF SPRINGS.

As it happens, the new opening hole is a fairly straightforward par 4, getting play under way satisfactorily, and it is followed by the first of five short holes, each one quite different from the rest. This green is raised up and surrounded by bunkers, with the steep cliff of Mount Rundle as an impressive backdrop. Then comes a good strategic par 5, played along a narrow fairway with Rundle's rock face on the right and bunkers to the left. These bunkers must be flirted with if there is to be any chance of finding the green in two, tucked away as it is round a corner to the right.

Short holes were clearly one of Stanley Thompson's great strengths. He built many world-class par 3s, the most famous of all being the Devil's Cauldron, now played as Banff's 4th. Everything is perfectly clear as the player stands on the tee. The green is some way below, sloping towards the player beyond a small glacial lake, surrounded by sand and grassy slopes leading up to the trees and rocks that frame the hole. It may look entirely natural, but the green-site was blasted out of the rocks, the creation of man and dynamite!

From here the course wends its way towards the Bow River and a wonderful sequence of riverside holes from the 8th to the 14th. Three of these are par 3s, but the 10th and 13th are substantially over 200 yards, quite a hefty clout from the back tees even today. Thompson's original 18th (now the 14th) was a terrific finisher, and it remains a great hole today, with two expansive nests of bunkers to be cleared on both the tee-shot and approach, the green itself right above the confluence of the Bow and Spray Rivers and only a few hundred feet from the tumbling Bow Falls. The 15th (already mentioned), is inspiring, the 16th and 17th are well-bunkered par 4s calling for good positional play, and the round ends with a stout par 5,

ELK ARE FREQUENT VISITORS TO THE FAIRWAYS AT BANFF SPRINGS.

AN ARM OF THE BOW RIVER MUST BE CARRIED TO FIND THE 10TH GREEN.

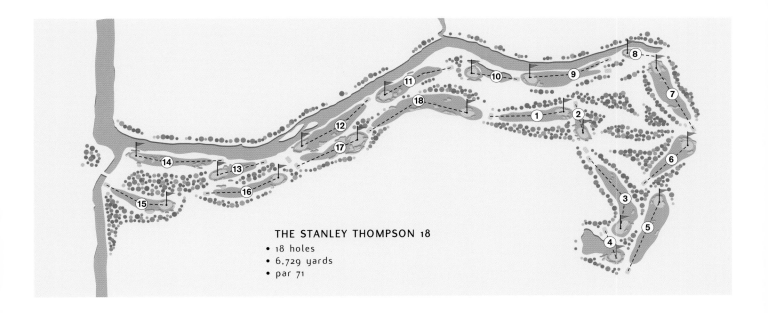

THE STANLEY THOMPSON 18
- 18 holes
- 6,729 yards
- par 71

characterized by Thompson's subtle use of moundwork and bunkering.

The hotel was designed by Bruce Price, one of the most prominent architects in New York in the late 19th century, as one of a string of luxury hotels along the Canadian Pacific Railway's route through the Rocky and Selkirk Mountains, with others at Lake Louise and Frontenac. The building underwent a complete restoration in 1928. Typical of the detailed planning that went into this operation was the commissioning of the furniture, specially made by a Montreal company as exact replicas of pieces found in the stately homes of Europe. So successful was this restoration that it raised the hotel to new heights of luxury and gained it an enviable reputation. In those days it was exclusively a summer resort, but in 1969 the decision was taken to keep it open all

year round, and winter sports are now as important a recreational activity as golf. Its 770 rooms and suites make this one of the world's biggest hotels, and with this immense capacity Banff Springs is an ideal venue as a conference centre, with world-class facilities and 2,100 square metres (23,000 square feet) of meeting space. The European-style spa, the Willow Stream, has been upgraded to keep it in the forefront of such facilities, and a health club and swimming pool help to ensure the wellbeing of guests, conference delegates, skiers, and golfers alike. Given the vast scale of the hotel, it comes as no surprise to find that its restaurants and bars offer an unrivalled diversity of culinary styles, culminating in the award-winning, five-star Banffshire Club. The Fairmont Banff Springs is truly on a scale to match its excellent surroundings.

Contact:

Fairmont Banff Springs
405 Spray Avenue
Banff
Alberta
Canada
T1L 1J4
Tel: +1 (403) 762 2211
Email: banffsprings@fairmont.com
www.fairmont.com/banffsprings

Fairmont Jasper Park Lodge,
Canada

It was Stanley Thompson's course at Jasper, built for the Canadian National Railway, that prompted their big rival, the Canadian Pacific Railway, to commission him to build a course for them at Banff Springs. That they are now united under one roof, Fairmont, is a cause for celebration. What these courses have in common (as well as their designer) is the fact that, because they were built for railway companies, it was possible to ship in thousands of tons of topsoil. This single factor enabled Thompson to create the best growing medium for grass in this climate of temperature extremes, to shape the holes to perfection, to build elevated tees, and to indulge in his favourite art of deceiving the golfer's eye.

Constructed in 1924–5, Jasper Park was a massive undertaking. More than 50 teams of horses and 200 men were needed simply to clear the site of boulders, rocks, and trees. Thompson's design was bold too, routing three holes (the 14th, 15th and 16th) around a peninsula jutting out into Lac Beauvert, a crystal-clear glacial lake. The course is set in a wide valley, surrounded by the high, snow-capped peaks of the Rockies, and Thompson took a good deal of inspiration for his design from them. Several of the fairways are aligned on a distant peak. Bunkers and moundwork often replicate or complement the skyline, and the freely available topsoil allowed him to scale these design features to the magnitude of the surroundings. From the moment it opened, Jasper was recognized as a masterpiece. Two of the greatest names in golf course architecture, Alister MacKenzie and George C. Thomas, visited the course in its early days, rating it among their very favourite designs. It was not just the romance of the place that they admired so much; they also respected the subtlety and strategy of the layout, the very features that distinguished their own work from the also-rans.

Bing Crosby, Marilyn Monroe, James Stewart, and Robert Mitchum were among the later celebrity visitors to Jasper, and Crosby (himself a very low handicap player) was one of many to appreciate the strengths of Thompson's course. Thompson's achievement here (and subsequently at Banff Springs) was a course that provides a continuous challenge for the good player, without over-facing the high-handicappers and occasional golfers who make up the majority of resort guests.

It is a frustration for golf historians that architect's plans for early courses rarely survive (if, indeed, there ever were actual plans). Happily, Thompson's original course blueprints for Jasper Park still exist, and they were used in 1994 when it was decided to restore the course. Restoration was carried out with painstaking care, particularly with regard to the tee boxes and bunkers. The bunkers themselves are worthy of study, with many of those guarding the greens set several yards (some as much as 60 yards) in front, although the way in which they are shaped makes them appear as though they are right in front, optically deceiving

the player into thinking that the green is nearer than it is. Those who are thus fooled, and drag or push their shot into one of these bunkers, will then find themselves faced with one of the most difficult shots to execute accurately, the medium-length or long bunker shot.

Straight hitting is required from the 1st tee (not always so easy to achieve at the start of the round), but the 2nd fairway is so wide that everyone will want to go for broke. It is a short par 5 on which many will fancy their chances — until they encounter Thompson's bunkers on the approach, that is. The 3rd swings to the right, a dog-leg on which the long hitter can drive out over the trees in an attempt to shorten the hole, and powerful golfers have an advantage on the 240-yard par-3 4th, one of two very substantial 'short' holes on the way out. Another short par 5 follows at the 5th, or par 4½ perhaps, because it is well within two-shot range for many golfers today. However, it is tightly bunkered and calls for arrow-like straightness on both long shots. Behind the green is a series of mounds and bunkers mimicking the outline of the mountains beyond. The 434-yard 8th is one of the toughest holes on the course, the drive being directed towards a fairway with a pronounced right-to-left slope. Even after a good landing, the approach to the bunkerless green will be blind, although it is easy enough to work out where the green is from the trees lining the fairway.

Two mounds in the shape of a buxom female form originally gave the 9th its name, Cleopatra. But Thompson himself removed them, not for any reasons of propriety, but rather in order to make the hole better. It is a 231-yard par 3 with a ring of bunkers defending the green on all sides. From the tee, the view beyond the green over the coniferous forests to the towering peaks is magnificent.

One of the joys of golf at Jasper Park is its tranquillity, each fairway progressing along its own private path. Although the surroundings remain constant, there is an ever-changing point of view as one hole succeeds another. At the 10th, a pond in front of the tee reflects the imposing mass of the mountains in the distance. Though not a threat for a competent golfer, farther on a host of bunkers on the right narrows the fairway at the length of a good drive. The 11th then strikes out towards Pyramid Mountain, its green being the hardest one to read on the entire course.

From here the course winds round the back of the woods, until on the 14th tee the golfer is confronted with a rather more serious carry over water, an arm of Lac Beauvert. This is not a long par 4 but it hugs the water all the way to the green, and the best approach is from as close to the water as possible. Then comes the shortest hole on the course, the 138-yard 15th, known as Bad Baby. One of the best short holes in golf, it has a tiny green perched on a mound.

WINTER SPORTS ARE A MAJOR ATTRACTION HERE. THE SKI LIFTS PROVIDE SPECTACULAR VISTAS ALSO FOR SUMMER VISITORS.

JASPER PARK'S 16TH GREEN IS LOCATED DANGEROUSLY CLOSE TO AN ARM OF LAC BEAUVERT.

FROM EVERY PART OF JASPER PARK THE VIEWS ARE SIMPLY BREATH-TAKING.

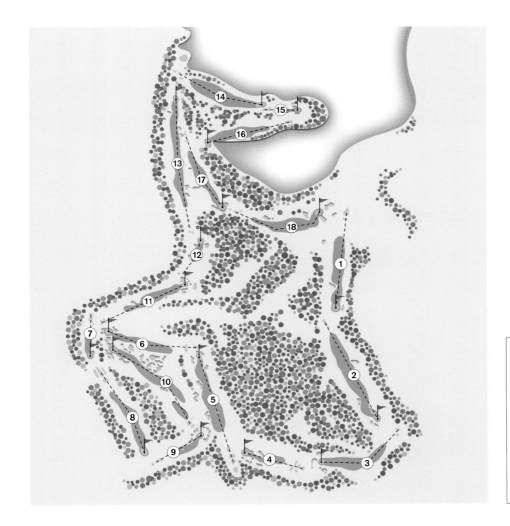

Contact:

The Fairmont Jasper Park Lodge
Old Lodge Road
Jasper
Alberta
Canada
ToE 1Eo
Tel: +1 (780) 852 3301
Email: jasperparklodge@fairmont.com
www.fairmont.com/jasper

Missing this green can lead to desperate recovery work. The 16th runs back along the peninsula, with another arm of the lake eating into the fairway just before the green. Jasper's 18th is another superb hole, with a curling, downhill fairway that favours the player who can draw the ball and control it, gaining many precious yards in the process and leaving an easier approach to a tightly bunkered green at the bottom of the hill.

Jasper Park offers 446 guest rooms and suites, some in the main lodge and others in nearby cabins. They have been carefully renovated to retain the spirit of the original lodge while being as up-to-date as possible. The views are, of course, stunning, both from the accommodation and from each of the dining rooms. For serious eating, the Edith Cavell Dining Room offers a true four-star experience with a considerable wine list.

Visitors from outside Canada will be intrigued by the Moose's Nook, which has a wine list of more than 60 Canadian wines not seen much outside the country, but are beginning to gain an international reputation. It is much less formal, and also offers live entertainment. There is also the spacious Beauvert Dining Room, overlooking the lake, while The Meadows Restaurant offers a bargain buffet breakfast.

Keltic Lodge/Highlands Links,
Nova Scotia, Canada

Cape Breton Highlands National Park is a particularly favoured part of Nova Scotia Island, overlooking the Gulf of St. Lawrence and the Atlantic Ocean. With a glorious mix of beaches and coastline, rivers, valleys, woods, and mountains it is blessed with great natural beauty and supports a wide variety of wildlife. Towards the end of the 1930s the National Park Services of Canada thought to bring tourists to the area by building a golf course, at the same time creating welcome employment for the local population. Wisely they sent for the doyen of Canadian golf course architects, Stanley Thompson, nicknamed the "Toronto Terror" on account of his flamboyant life style.

THE APPROACH TO THE 15TH GREEN IS PLAYED TOWARDS A BACKDROP OF WHALE ISLAND AND THE ATLANTIC OCEAN.

It might be thought that anyone given such a fecund site could hardly fail to produce a masterpiece. Unfortunately, the world of golf is full of dull courses which completely overlook the design potential of their location and the opportunities for imaginative holes provided by their unique topography. Highlands Links, on the other hand, is an object lesson in what can be achieved by an architect with vision who takes his inspiration from the ground on which he is working: "Nature must always be the architect's model," said Thompson. And for the first-time visitor the initial impression is of a stroll through rolling woodland with occasional excursions to the hills or the beach with a golf club in hand. Thompson does not lay his design hand open on the table. Instead he uses it with guile, luring the golfer into many an unsuspected trap in the process. This sense of oneness with the surrounding world is further enhanced by the Highlands Links' enhancement and protection of its wildlife and natural habitats through its active membership of the Audubon Society, which is dedicated to a major programme of habitat and environmental management and conservation.

A golf course in such a remote spot is not likely to attract many visitors unless it can offer good on-site accommodation; the Keltic Lodge was built at the same time as the course. In contrast with the other Canadian resorts featured in this book, the Keltic Lodge is intimate, rather in the style of a good English country pub. The lodge itself has 32 guest rooms, with a further 40 in the adjoining inn, as well as self-contained bungalows. Seafood and local produce take pride of place on the menus of its two restaurants, the Purple Thistle and the Atlantic. The cuisine is a mix of native Canadian with European influences, and includes lobster, mussels, wild salmon, and other fish and meats as fresh as can be.

Inevitably the natural world is the focus of non-golfing activities at Ingonish Beach, with many different walks and trails through the woods or along the shore. Whale watching is very popular, and especially good when the viewing party is small enough to fit on to a local fishing boat. More energetic pastimes include sea and river fishing, mountain-and trail-biking, sea kayaking and tennis.

THE 6TH GREEN, SURROUNDED BY WILD FLOWERS, WITH THE CLYBURN BROOK IN THE BACKGROUND.

Part of the charm of Keltic Lodge lies in getting there. The drive from Sydney or Halifax is a pleasure in itself, following the Cabot Trail with its traditional fishing villages and ever changing scenery. Thus, visitors absorb the atmosphere at a gentle pace. As the journey comes to an end, the road passes the last hole of Highlands Links Golf Course — and a sense of anticipation sets in.

Following a multi-million dollar renovation programme in 1995, Highlands Links today is presented in tip-top condition, as befits such a distinguished course. It is not long but its quality shines through, despite Thompson's skill at camouflaging

artifice to make it all seem totally natural. One of the aspects of the course that underlines this is the unevenness of the early and late fairways, replicating the humps and bumps which give such diverse lies in the traditional links golf of the British coasts. Those brought up on level, smooth fairways will find this difficult, perhaps even unfair, but to acquire the skills needed to flight a ball properly from such a lie, probably in the wind, is one of the greatest joys in golf.

As early as the opening hole it becomes apparent just why card length is not everything. At just over 400 yards this is — on paper — only a mid-length par 4,

but the fairway is crinkled, stances can be awkward, and both shots are played uphill, very probably into the wind. It may take a good player two of his best shots to make the green. Thompson's family was Scottish and all the holes here bear Scottish names. Tam O'Shanter is the name of the 2nd hole, apparently because the shape of the green reminded him of the traditional Scottish headgear. It is a great example of a bunkerless hole, the folds, depressions and rises of the fairway providing all the defence needed. The views out to the right, towards the ocean, are enticing, and this hole gradually falls towards a green set in idyllic fashion alongside the shore.

PUTTING ON THE 3RD GREEN.

Although the par-3 3rd is played over a lake, the green is well back from the water and only a really terrible shot will perish. Heich O'Fash is the name of the 4th hole, meaning "heap of trouble." It is a name shared with the 9th hole on the King's Course at Gleneagles, and there is a certain visual similarity between the two, with their greens set up on nobs behind bunkers against a backdrop of mountains. The Highlands Links' version is only 325 yards long, but high scores are not uncommon even among low handicappers. The 165-yard 5th is called Canny Slap, referring to the manner in which the golfer should aim to the left of the green to allow the ball to feed downhill towards the flag.

An unusual feature of Highlands Links is its two excellent back-to-back par 5s on each half, the 6th hole featuring a wicked drive across water to reach the angled fairway, and the 7th hole taking play into the hills and tumbling ground of a different nature. The 8th continues the journey, plunging downhill to a picture-postcard green, and the next few holes run in and out of a river valley at the far end of the course. There is a long walk from the 12th to 13th along the Clyburn Brook, but in this context it seems entirely reasonable — not merely a nature ramble — and something of a respite before the rigours of the demanding 13th, with its tight drive to a sloping fairway, demanding excellent ball control from the tee.

THE CHARACTER CHANGES AT THE FAR END OF THE COURSE. THIS IS THE 7TH GREEN.

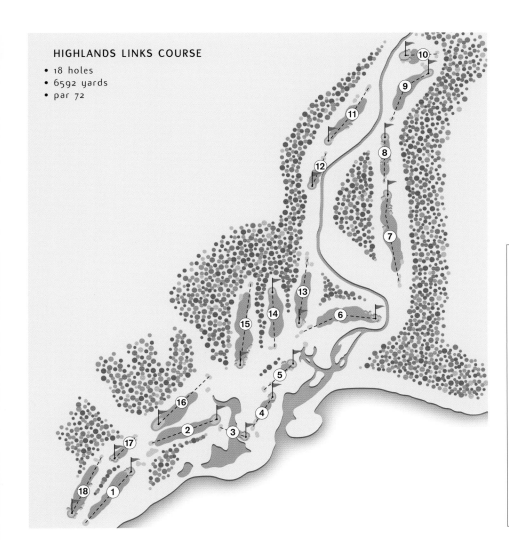

HIGHLANDS LINKS COURSE

- 18 holes
- 6592 yards
- par 72

Contact:

The Keltic Lodge
Middle Head Peninsula
Ingonish Beach
Nova Scotia
Canada
Tel: +1 (902) 285 2880
(From USA) Toll Free: 1 800 565 0444
Email: keltic@signatureresorts.com
http://signatureresorts.com/index.asp

Highlands Links
Cape Breton Highlands National Park
Ingonish Beach
Nova Scotia
Canada
Tel: 1-800-441-1118
Email: highlands.links@pc.gc.ca
www.highlandslinksgolf.com

It says a great deal for the par-5 15th that, even in this stellar company, it stands out from the rest by a whisker. Big hitters are invited to drive out over a shoulder of land, perilously close to trees on the left, to get many extra yards of roll and the chance to get on the green easily in two. The absolutely stunning view seen when walking down the hill towards the green, out over the ocean to Whale Island in the distance, is truly memorable. From here the course returns parallel to the 1st and 2nd, the 18th making a nicely strategic hole on which to finish, with a drive which successfully avoids the bunker on the left of the fairway setting up by far the better approach to the green, with trouble just off the putting surface to the right in the form of a big bunker and a road. In the end, 6,592 yards of this sort of golf is so much more rewarding than 7,592 yards of indifferent design.

Peninsula Papagayo Four Seasons Resort, Costa Rica

Very little is known of Costa Rica's history before 1502, the year in which it was "discovered" by Christopher Columbus. During the 17 days he spent there, Columbus was particularly taken with the friendliness of the local people and also with their gold ornaments, which suggested to him the name costa rica, or "rich coast". The Spanish subsequently invaded in the hope of finding huge quantities of gold, but their quest proved fruitless, and Costa Rica was largely forgotten about until 1808, when coffee growing began. Soon entrepreneurs moved in, the country acquired a wealthy class and politics began to gain a foothold. Although there were power struggles among the rich coffee growers they had the foresight to establish the country as an independent state with democratic elections. Importantly, the constitution of 1949 dismantled the country's armed forces, and living in peace has been a cornerstone of this truly friendly nation ever since. Coupled with this is Costa Rica's national commitment to nature conservation, making it stand out as an oasis of calm far removed from its less stable neighbouring countries.

No less than 27 per cent of Costa Rica is protected land, and national parks cover 12 per cent of the country. Its jungles contain 1500 different tree species and 850 species of bird, plus monkeys, sloths, tapirs, armadillos, and jaguar. Costa Rica is a nature-lover's paradise, and this is reflected in its tourism industry.

Nature lies at the heart of many of the magical excursions from the brand new Four Seasons Resort at Papagayo on Costa Rica's Pacific coast. For instance, the rafting trips up the Corobici and Tenorio Rivers are likely to yield sightings of howler monkeys, iguanas, osprey, tiger herons and motmots. The Parque Nacional Rincón de la Vieja, a two hour drive away, is a 14,000-hectare (35,000-acre) national park in which over 350 species of bird have been observed. It also contains the Rincón Volcano, one of the more gently active of Costa Rica's volcanoes. Here — and elsewhere — it is possible to take a Canopy Tour, walking high up at tree-top level in the rainforest, and the mineral-rich mud of the park's natural volcanic thermal spa is wonderfully cleansing and refreshing for the skin. At Los Inocentes Ecological Ranch, toucans, monkeys, and sloths may be seen from horseback, and the wildlife of the tropical dry forest can be observed from horseback close to the resort. A catamaran is available for guests to explore the ocean wildlife, and crocodiles are one of the attractions at Palo Verde Wildlife Park, where a flat-bottomed boat is the mode of transport through saltwater and freshwater lagoons and marshes, mangrove swamps, and savannah woodland.

For those with more active tastes, there is high-quality surfing for experienced surfers on the beaches at Witch's Rock, Petrero Grande, and Ollie's Point, while beginners and the moderately able are catered for at Tamarindo, on the south side of the Gulf of Papagayo. Scuba diving is popular, as well as windsurfing, snorkelling, kayaking, and white-water rafting. The resort has a spa and fitness centre, and there are tennis courts both on site and locally. Deep-sea fishing for marlin, Pacific sailfish, wahoo, tuna, and dorado is available, and the resort also arranges big-game fishing up to 65 km (40 miles) off shore. Encouragingly for fish stocks, the Four Seasons requests that all not-for-eating fish be released back into the waters.

ONLY A PRECISELY HIT SHOT WILL SUFFICE ON THE PRETTY 7TH HOLE.

STUNNING VIEWS ABOUND AT PAPAGAYO. THIS IS THE PAR-3 5TH.

The 165 guest rooms, with views out over the ocean or inland over the gardens or forest, all have a private terrace or balcony and range up to the impressive three-bedroom Presidential Suite. Formal dining is in the Di Mare restaurant, with both indoor and outdoor seating, and Italian dishes and seafood featuring prominently on the menu. The Papagayo restaurant offers more casual dining, and Congo's is a pool- and beachside bar and grill which stages theme nights on Wednesdays, Fridays, and Saturdays. Ten minutes away, at the golf club, Caracol is an informal snack-lunch bar which turns into a steak house in the evening. *Caracol* is Spanish for conch, and the architecture of the clubhouse is inspired by the elaborate shell of this tasty mollusc.

The golf course opened in February 2004, and was designed by Arnold Palmer and his company. Although there are majestic ocean views from 14 holes, this is not a seaside course; rather, it rises and falls through a lush tropical forest. Nor is it a long course by today's standards — only 6,788 yards from the very back — but, in order to take maximum advantage of the architectural potential of the site, and in order not to damage the sensitive ecology, the routing leaves some quite large distances from one green to the next tee. This is certainly a riding course, and not one for walking. But then, with daytime temperatures remaining

consistently high throughout the year (25–35°C or 77–93°F), it may be wise to restrict physical exertion to a minimum.

It is a drive of several hundred yards from the clubhouse to the practice range, but that is conveniently close to the 1st tee – or, more precisely, tees, for Palmer has put in multiple tees to allow the course to be played by golfers of a wide range of abilities. This 1st is a par-5

double dog-leg, swinging first right then left, bunkered only on the right of the drive landing area, and again on the right of the approach to the green. All the holes have names, the 2nd being Tiburon, Spanish for shark. A short hole of modest length, it is played across rough ground to a green angled from right to left, with what might be described as the shark's "fin" protruding on the right to embrace a circular bunker. When the pin is cut on the back left, in

the shark's mouth as it were, only the supremely confident (or supremely foolish) aim for it. From the 2nd green there is quite a long drive through the forest, before the 3rd, Buena Vista, is laid out before the golfer. In a following wind, this shortish par 4 might be driven by the low handicapper. However, Palmer has built in plenty of risk, with a tree directly in line off the tee and two sets of expansive bunkers short of and alongside the green.

The 4th is a par 5 of moderate length (538 yards from the back), with a fairway which turns sharply to the left at the length of a good drive. Strong hitters will need their tee shot to carry bunkers in the crook of the dog-leg, at least 270 yards from the back. There are also bunkers straight ahead for the golfer who prefers not to risk the left-hand route.

Water has not been used excessively at Papagayo, but it is pressed into very effective service on the par-3 5th, La Poza (the pool), where a large expanse of water must be carried between tee and green. With the green angled off to the right, alongside the pool, a very controlled high fade would be ideal, but there is precious little margin for error. At 446 yards, the 6th is the only substantial par 4 on the front nine. Helpfully, the fairway slopes downhill, and long hitters have to be careful not to run out of fairway. All players need to take great care approaching the green which slopes away from the shot at the rear of the putting surface. It is then another lengthy excursion through the forest to find the 7th tee, which looks out over a wonderful vista. Closer to hand, however, the green is sited on the side of a hill on the far side of a deep valley. There is no room for inaccuracy, and the penalty for a topped shot does not bear thinking about! The drive to the next tee is perhaps the longest yet, while that following the 9th is serious motoring, taking the golfer off onto a completely separate tract of land, with

THE APPROACH TO THE PAR-4 15TH MUST CLEAR A STREAM IMMEDIATELY IN FRONT OF THE GREEN.

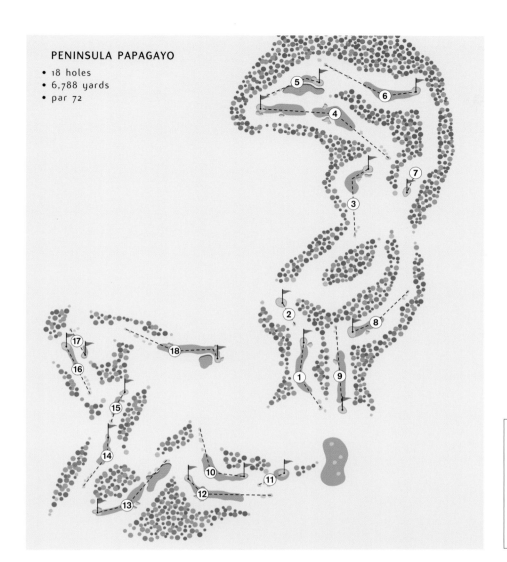

PENINSULA PAPAGAYO

- 18 holes
- 6,788 yards
- par 72

Contact:

Four Seasons Resort Costa Rica
Peninsula de Papagayo
Guanacaste
Costa Rica
Tel: +506 696 0000
www.fourseasons.com/costarica/index.html

the 10th and 11th taking play up towards the practice range.

Now the course is lengthening, and the 12th is the longest hole of all, a monster par 5 of 601 yards. The 13th, too, is seriously long as par 4s go, at 468 yards, and the approach to the green is all the way uphill. High handicappers may also

be concerned at the compulsory water carry from the tee. But that is the end of the big hitting for the time being, with the next three holes, all two-shotters, becoming progressively shorter. The par-3 17th is only a mid-iron shot at most. Palmer was a dashing golfer, and never one to duck a challenge. His 18th at Papagayo is a great gambler's hole.

It is a par 5 of 550 yards, the sort of length today's top golfers expect to reach in two shots every time. What Palmer has done is to bend the fairway sharply to the right, around a lake, on the approach to the green. Can the player be sure of carrying the water all the way to the green? Why play safe at a time like this?

Casa de Campo, Dominican Republic

When the history of golf course architecture in the 20th century comes to be written, it is likely that Pete Dye will be awarded the accolade of the most innovative and influential architect working in the last quarter of the century. Born in Ohio, he was a good amateur golfer who as a young man was a very successful insurance salesman. By his mid-thirties he had made enough money to leave that profession and set up as a golf course architect. His break-through into the big time came in 1969, when the Harbour Town Golf Links opened in South Carolina. At a time when many new golf courses were formulaic and bland in the extreme, this collaboration with Jack Nicklaus (then at the peak of his playing powers) immediately caught the attention of knowledgable golfers with its refreshing individuality. Harbour Town has kept its place in the golf rankings ever since, despite the arrival of so many newer courses, and is the regular home of the Heritage, one of the most popular events on the USPGA Tour, always attracting a star field.

The following year, Dye was invited to construct "a special course" near the town of La Romana, on the southeast coast of the Dominican Republic, as part of a 2,800-hectare (7,000-acre) luxury resort complex being developed by Alvaro Carta. Dye went up in an aeroplane and eventually spotted a promising 5-km (3-mile) stretch of coastline which to him suggested a potentially stunning golf course, but to the rest of us would merely have looked like a jumble of rocks and undergrowth. A workforce of 300 men cleared the site using machetes. Then they made their own topsoil, using a mixture of sand, dirt and *cachaza*, an organic by-product of sugar refining. This had to be spread by hand before the grass could be planted – not as seed, but as individual sprigs. Several tees and greens were built out into the sea, requiring retaining walls. These were made using a local coral called *dientes del perro*, or teeth of the dog, from which this inaugural course derived its name. Dye described the opportunity as "a chance of a lifetime to create a seaside course where so much of the sea – almost three miles of it – came into play." On six holes the golfer is

required to play over the sea. Dye returned a few years later to add a second course, the Links. This is somewhat shorter at 6,461 yards, but there are five holes on which water is a threat and the gently hilly ground is used cleverly to affect strategy. Newest of the three courses is Dye Fore, a 7,770-yard monster roaming inland to give superb views of the Chavón River, the village of Altos de Chavón, the mountains and the Caribbean. Packing a considerable punch, it makes a fine contrast to Teeth of the Dog.

Casa de Campo is almost a town in itself, centred on the main hotel, in which accommodation is in guest rooms and suites. Villas are scattered around the resort, some privately owned, and others available for resort guests, family parties or even business retreats. A variety of restaurants throughout the resort covers almost every culinary taste, from sandwiches and pizzas to *filet mignon* and *churrasco*, via Italy, Mexico, China, and Japan. Catamaran cruises and day trips to Santo Domingo and La Romana give a flavour of Dominican geography and history (which goes back to the time of Christopher Columbus).

PETE DYE'S BRILLIANT ROUTING OF THE TEETH OF THE DOG COURSE PROVIDES MANY MAGICAL GREEN SETTINGS.

THE 5TH ON THE TEETH OF THE DOG COURSE IS A LONG
PAR 3 REQUIRING A FULL CARRY OVER THE SEA.

Nearer at hand is the extraordinary village of Altos de Chavón, constructed in 1976 in the style of a European settlement of the 16th or 17th century, with cobbled streets, a church dedicated to St. Stanislaus, and even a 5,000-seat open-air amphitheatre in the Greek style. Built using traditional craft techniques, it houses the studios of potters, ceramicists, and artists in silk and woven fibre, as well as a school of design, the regional museum of archaeology, and artist-in-residence programmes. Supporting the entire project is the Altos de Chavón Cultural Centre Foundation.

Riding is an important activity at Casa de Campo, with trail riding through the sugar plantations or by the Chavón River into the tropical forest. Jumping horses

are available, as are no fewer than 80 polo ponies: matches are played weekly during the season, which runs from November to April. Other facilities include a shooting centre, a tennis centre, swimming pools, a private beach, a running trail, a fitness centre, and bicycle hire. Sea and river fishing can be arranged, and other waterborne activities include scuba diving, kayaking, windsurfing, and paddle boats. It goes without saying that there is also a spa to soothe away the aches and pains provoked by over-activity.

Like many good golf course architects, Dye made an extensive study of the classic links courses of Scotland before starting out on his second career. His

style has been summed up as "pot bunkers and railway sleepers (railroad ties)", but that is very much an over-simplification. There are, however, passing references to Scotland on Teeth of the Dog: the 2nd hole, for instance, was influenced by the final hole at historic Prestwick, scene of the first 12 Open Championships (and 24 in all). Charles Blair Macdonald, one of the founding fathers of American course design, also visited Scotland (back in the late 19th century), and according to Dye the 3rd hole, a par 5, simulates Macdonald's own style. Another founding father of American design was Donald Ross, the Scottish émigré who designed many classic American courses, and the 4th at

MULTIPLE TEES ALLOW TEETH OF THE DOG TO BE PLAYED AT A PRACTICABLE LENGTH BY GOLFERS OF VARYING ABILITIES.

THE RUGGED, INLAND SETTING OF THE DYE FORE COURSE — A SPLENDID FOIL FOR ITS TWO COMPANION COURSES.

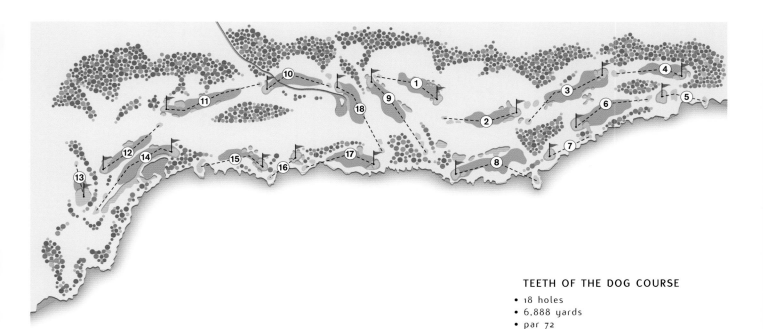

TEETH OF THE DOG COURSE
- 18 holes
- 6,888 yards
- par 72

Casa de Campo, a short downhill par 4, was modelled on his 3rd hole on Pinehurst's No 2 course.

Then begins the first sequence of holes played alongside and over the Caribbean. The 5th is a substantial par 3, significantly over 200 yards, on which the green slopes away from the sea, calling for a delicately drawn tee-shot. After the long two-shot 6th comes another exciting par 3, the 7th, with nothing between tee and green except beach and bunker. From the 8th tee, built far out into the sea, the drive is played over sea and sand to an angled fairway, and then the approach must be fired at a green standing right at the water's edge. It is a great set of holes, and there is just as good still to come.

Five inland holes take play to the far end of the course before the sea is encountered once again on the par-5 14th, which plays round a salt-water lagoon to the green. The 15th is almost the 8th in reverse and generally plays into the wind, making it one of the more testing holes on the course. Another short hole played across the waves follows, and then comes the last skirmish with the sea. From the 17th tee the golfer is invited to go for broke: the longer the drive, the easier the hole becomes. That, of course, means that the drive must flirt with the sea, and just the tiniest touch of fade will see the ball disappear into the water. It is a fine risk-and-reward hole. The final hole takes play back inland, a sturdy par 4 on which the second shot is played to a green protected by a pond and a long bunker on the left.

Contact:

Casa de Campo
PO Box 140
La Romana
Dominican Republic
Tel: +1 809 523 3333 or +1-809 523 8698
Email: reserva@ccampo.com.do
www.casadcampo.com

Liverpool and the Lancashire Coast, England

At first sight, the city of Liverpool may not seem an obvious place to golf. Yet it is an ideal base for exploring some of the great venues of Open Championship golf, as well as a number of other first-rate and historic courses. Conveniently, most of these courses are easily reached by rail. Royal Birkdale, Royal Liverpool, and Royal Lytham and St. Anne's are the famous Open Championship courses, and they keep close company with Formby, Hillside, Southport and Ainsdale, West Lancashire, Wallasey, Caldy, and Heswall. Together they make for a long and impressive list.

There is more to life than golf, of course, and Liverpool offers plenty for everyone. Today's busy city was nothing more than a mere fishing village until the 18th century when it began to grow into a port, eventually becoming Europe's greatest Atlantic seaport. The big shipping lines erected imposing docks and head offices, endowing Liverpool with an impressive Victorian and Edwardian waterfront imbued with a powerful sense of unity and purpose. Now the big ocean liners are no more. But the impressive waterfront remains, and is now home to designer shops, a branch of the Tate Gallery, an excellent maritime museum, and fine restaurants.

Behind the waterfront the ground rises towards Hope Street, an appropriately named street if ever there was one because it links Liverpool's two cathedrals. At one end is the monumental Anglican cathedral, second in size only to St. Peter's in Rome, and at the other the more modern Roman Catholic cathedral with its conical roof rising like a beacon over Liverpool. Between the two stands the Philharmonic Hall, home to the Royal Liverpool Philharmonic Orchestra, one of Britain's oldest and finest. Other attractions include the Walker Art Gallery, the City Museums, the splendid neoclassical St. George's Hall, a flourishing Chinatown, Aintree Race Course (home of the Grand National), Liverpool and Everton Football Clubs, and the Beatles Story Museum and Magical Mystery Tour.

Next to the Royal Liver Building, overlooking the Pier Head right by Prince's Dock, is the Crowne Plaza Liverpool, a modern (1998) hotel that is both comfortable and close to all the city has to offer. It is not a resort — it does not pretend to be — yet both the hotel and its restaurant have won awards, and the smart restaurants and bars of the Albert Dock are no more than a gentle stroll away.

The Royal Liverpool Golf Club is one of the oldest English seaside links, founded in 1869, and lies on the westernmost tip of the Wirral, a broad spit of land jutting out into the Irish Sea between the estuaries of the Rivers Dee and Mersey. This was once the site of the racecourse of the Liverpool Hunt Club, so it should come as no surprise to find that the golf course is remarkably flat, with none of the giant dunes of, say, Sandwich or Birkdale. It should not be imagined for a moment, however, that this flatness makes it any easier to play — far from it. The club hosted the inaugural Amateur Championship in 1885 and its first Open Championship in 1897, and it has been testing the techniques and nerves of fields of world-class golfers ever since, and in 2006 it welcomes the Open Championship once more. The test of skill begins right on the 1st tee, with a drive to a bunkerless fairway on which it is possible to go out-of-bounds to the left and to the right. On the right is a grassy bank — a cop — which separates the fairway from the practice ground; on the left are the clubhouse and a line of gardens. Almost invariably played into the wind, it makes a formidable opener, and a great 19th-hole decider in match-play.

ROYAL BIRKDALE HAS PLAYED HOST TO EIGHT OPEN CHAMPIONSHIPS. THE PROFESSIONALS DEEM IT TO BE THE FAIREST COURSE ON THE OPEN ROSTER.

ROYAL LYTHAM'S CLUBHOUSE OVERLOOKS THE 18TH GREEN OF THIS VERY TESTING LINKS.

From here play moves around the centre of the course in a way which brings the wind from a different angle on every shot. The wind is a considerable factor on the drive at the 6th, a terrifying hole into the teeth of a stiff breeze. A hedge eats into the fairway 200 yards out. It simply must be carried! Reaching the 8th green (a hole on which even the great Bobby Jones came unstuck in his famous 1930 Impregnable Quadrilateral), the ground is now more rolling, and from the 9th to the 12th there is a lovely stretch of holes overlooking the Welsh and Lancashire coasts and Hilbre Island. A good score is by no means

certain at this point in the round, but the finish from the 14th is exceptionally demanding, 2,432 yards at an average of 486 yards for each of those five holes.

Next oldest of the Open Championship courses in the area is Royal Lytham and St. Anne's. Like Royal Liverpool, it does not fit the stereotypical image of a championship links. It most certainly is, however, although the sea is not visible from the course. Fearsomely bunkered, Lytham calls for wise course management as it gradually turns the screw. A 206-yard par 3 is an unusual opener and, with two

more short holes to come on the outward nine, low scores are not uncommon. Strokes start to slip away from the 12th, the only short hole on the back nine, and the 15th and 17th are two of the most demanding par 4s in England.

The Open Championship did not come to Royal Birkdale until 1954, making this course a comparative youngster, although it has been a regular host ever since. Here the dunes are impressive, mountainous even, and for the most part the fairways thread through the valleys between them. This gives spectators grand viewing, and

ACTION FROM THE 2004 CURTIS CUP MATCH AT FORMBY, IN WHICH THE AMERICAN LADIES TRIUMPHED 10-8 IN AN EXCITING CONTEST.

the level fairways professionals view as the fairest on the Open roster. Birkdale does not have any world-famous holes, but has no weaknesses either, and all 18 holes combine to provide a stiff yet utterly fair test. The thrill of driving over a wilderness of dunes and gorse from the elevated 18th tee to a split and bunker-ridden fairway, with Birkdale's unique ocean-liner-like clubhouse in the distance, provides a fitting climax to a demanding course.

Separated from Royal Birkdale by only a footpath, Hillside Golf Club enjoys similarly impressive dunes, and on the relatively modern back nine the course climbs on and off them in stunning fashion. Stands of tall pines frame several holes, making this a particularly photogenic course. The 11th and 17th, parallel par 5s, are perhaps the most scenic of all the holes. Southport and Ainsdale also adjoins Hillside, separated from it this time by a railway. It is an old James Braid course, again links, with a particularly notable par-5 16th hole, Gumbleys. Two exciting Ryder Cups were played here in 1933 and 1937, with honours spread evenly between the US and Great Britain and Ireland teams.

Heading south, there is a slight golfing gap (only a mile or two) before reaching Formby, by far the prettiest of these renowned links courses. Hidden away from the public gaze by pine forests (a rare English home to the endangered red squirrel), it is one of those places where the visitor feels very privileged to be. Over the years it has seen international

TIGER WOODS IN ACTION DURING THE 2001 OPEN CHAMPIONSHIP AT ROYAL LYTHAM.

ROYAL LIVERPOOL COURSE

- 18 holes
- 7,165 yards
- par 72

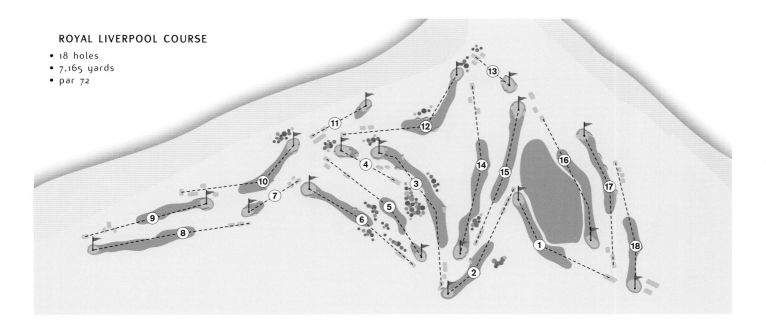

golf at high amateur level, most recently in the 2004 Curtis Cup. In the past the dunes here have suffered from coastal erosion, and new holes were added some years ago when others were lost. These come around the turn and are among the most memorable holes on a very memorable course, star billing perhaps going to the double dog-leg par-5 8th, a brilliantly strategic bunkerless hole. Contained within the championship course is another, that of Formby Ladies' Golf Club, one of only three ladies' clubs in England with a delightful links course.

At Blundellsands, home to the West Lancashire Golf Club, the wild Lancashire dunes give way to Liverpudlian urbanity. Established in 1873, this very old club, the oldest surviving club in Lancashire, is twinned with Royal Montreal, which was founded in the same year. The dunes here are not so imposing as those further north, yet the ground has enough movement to make this an exacting test for golfers of all standards. It has been a regular final qualifying course for Birkdale Opens, and will be so again now that Royal Liverpool is back on the Open roster.

Three further Wirral courses are worthy of attention. Heswall is a charming parkland course looking out over the salt-marshes of the Dee Estuary to the hills of Flintshire in North Wales. Its neighbour, Caldy, boasts an enticing mix of downland, parkland and links holes within its 18 holes. Again, the views from its fairways are to be savoured. Finally, there is the fine links course at Wallasey, one of England's hidden gems and a place of lofty dunes, bouncing fairways, secretive greens and dramatic seascapes.

Golf in and around Liverpool

Crowne Plaza Liverpool
St Nicholas Place, Princes Dock, Pier Head,
Liverpool L3 1QW
England
Tel: +44 (0)151 243 8000
Email: enquiries@cpliverpool.com
www.cpliverpool.com

Royal Liverpool Golf Club
Meols Drive, Hoylake,
Wirral CH47 4AL
England
Tel: +44 (0)151 632 3101
Email: sec@royal-liverpool-golf.com
www.royal-liverpool-golf.com

Royal Lytham and St. Annes Golf Club
Links Gate, Lytham St. Annes,
Lancashire FY8 3LQ
England
Tel: +44 (0)1253 724206
Email: bookings@royallytham.org
www.royallytham.org

Stoke Park and the Surrey Heathland, England

The earliest golf in the British Isles was played in medieval Scotland, on links beside the sea. Scots later came south with King James VI of Scotland when he ascended the English throne as James I in 1603, bringing the game with them, and by 1608 golf was played regularly on Blackheath, southeast of London. Little more is known of the history of golf in England until the 1860s, when several clubs were established, including the London Scottish on Wimbledon Common. Other clubs followed, but it soon became clear that their courses, on heavy inland soil, did not really offer the same playing characteristics as the fast-running links on the sandy shoreline of Scotland. It was the establishment in 1893 of a club at Woking, about 50 km (30 miles) south-west of London, that opened the eyes of keen players to the golfing potential of Surrey. A vast sandbelt runs through the county, spreading also into Berkshire, Hampshire, and West Sussex, and so well drained that it grows little other than gorse, heather, and the sort of fine turf that might be found within earshot of breaking waves. This was the discovery that changed the nature of inland golf in Britain for good.

As it happened, this period was also the heyday of railway expansion. City lawyers, bankers, insurance brokers, and stockbrokers found that they could now afford to move out of London and live in the peace and quiet of the countryside and commute to their offices in an hour by train. As golf in England was very much a middle-class affair (unlike in Scotland) these were the very men who happened to be in the right place at the right time to found golf clubs, which were frequently associated with a particular profession. Thus Woking was for many years linked with the law, and Walton Heath with the press. Some of these clubs — Sunningdale, Wentworth, and Walton Heath, for instance — have gone on to earn international reputations. Others, such as New Zealand and Swinley Forest, have deliberately maintained a very low profile, their lucky members preferring to play their golf in peace and quiet, without the disruptions of professional tournaments or corporate events. What is more, nearly all of these courses were laid out in the years before the First World War, and most of them have remained reasonably unaltered to this day.

Almost all the great names of the golden age of English golf course design are represented in these courses, with Alister Mackenzie being perhaps the only notable absentee. The biggest name is Harry Colt, who was also Secretary of Sunningdale and handily placed to advise on layouts in the area, such as at Swinley Forest, St. George's Hill, Wentworth West and East courses and Camberley Heath. Both courses at Walton Heath and the Berkshire are the work of Herbert Fowler, while James Braid laid out North Hants and Hankley Common. Tom Simpson designed New Zealand, J.H. Taylor Royal Mid-Surrey, J.F. Abercromby Coombe Hill, Worplesdon and the Addington, while Willie Park first laid out Sunningdale and West Hill. Mention should also be made of Liphook on the Hampshire-Sussex border, the only known course designed by Arthur Croome, and a little gem. Nearby, Blackmoor is another Colt course, and finally, no list of first-rate heathland courses would be complete without West Sussex near Pulborough, the furthest south of them all, designed by Sir Guy Campbell and C.K. Hutchison, and an absolute beauty. It is an extraordinary list.

THE IMPRESSIVE 18TH CENTURY MANSION AT THE HUB OF STOKE PARK.

THE 7TH HOLE ON WENTWORTH'S WEST COURSE.

Sunningdale's Old Course has had a distinguished history as a tournament venue, as well as being one of the loveliest of places for social play. In recent years it has staged the Walker Cup, the European Open, and the Weetabix Women's British Open. It was laid out on a barren heath, but thousands of oaks, birches, and pines have grown over the 100 years since

it was opened, and these days it is more of a woodland course. There are more open spaces and more heather on the New Course, another Colt design, added in 1923. Each course is as good as the other and the pair of them make for a wonderful day's golf. It is rare to find a club with two courses of such equal standing, yet there are several others in the area: Wentworth's West and

East Courses, the Berkshire's Red and Blue Courses and Walton Heath's Old and New Courses. Riches indeed!

It would be quite feasible to play all these from a hotel base in London, but why not avoid the traffic and stay out of town in a resort that yields nothing in quality or amenities to the best London hotels? Conveniently located near to Heathrow Airport, just off the M25, M4, and M40, is the Stoke Park Club. The clubhouse and golf course will be familiar to all James Bond aficionados, as they feature in two Bond films, *Goldfinger* and *Tomorrow Never Dies*, but the club's pedigree is much longer than that and very prestigious. The estate is known to have remained in the same family from 1066 to 1581, when it was sold to the Crown to pay off the debts incurred by the Earl of Huntingdon. Elizabeth I visited the manor, and Charles I was imprisoned there before his trial and execution. In the 18th century John Penn, grandson of William Penn, founder of Pennsylvania, returned to England and bought the estate. The manor was too dilapidated to be inhabited, so he had most of it demolished and a new mansion built by James Wyatt, architect to George III. Frequently likened to an iced wedding cake, the building is set off by its grounds, laid out by Lancelot "Capability" Brown and Humphry Repton, two of the most famous landscape gardeners of all time. The estate remained in private hands until 1908, when it was bought by Nick "Pa" Lane Jackson, founder of the

BOTH COURSES AT WALTON HEATH WERE LAID OUT BY HERBERT FOWLER, WHO ALSO DESIGNED EASTWARD HO IN MASSACHUSETTS.

THE DOWNHILL, PAR-3 13TH ON THE OLD COURSE AT SUNNINGDALE.

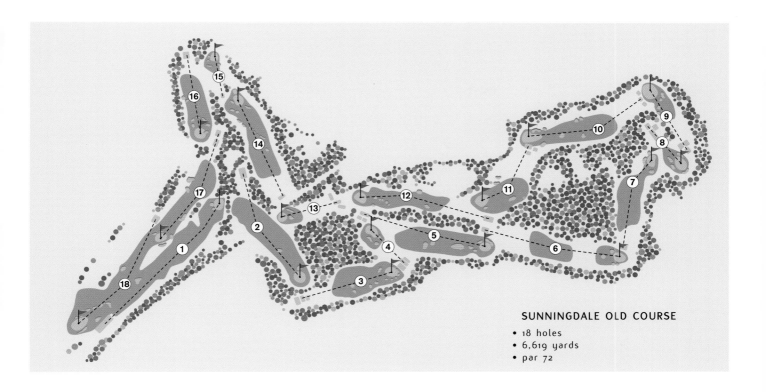

SUNNINGDALE OLD COURSE

- 18 holes
- 6,619 yards
- par 72

Corinthian Sporting Club, the greatest amateur sporting association of its age. He commissioned Harry Colt to lay out a golf course within the grounds and, although not all of Colt's work survived the creation of a further 9 holes, all the classics remain, especially the short 7th, said to have been the model for Mackenzie's 12th at Augusta National. Much restoration has been done to the course since and it is always maintained in superb condition.

The mansion has also been restored, and Stoke Park offers members and non-members a choice of 21 beautifully furnished rooms and suites. Because it is so small, its service is a matter of great pride. Good taste is a given and, whether for formal dining in the Park Restaurant or for more casual occasions in the Orangery, the surroundings create an elegant ambience for fine food and wine. Quality shows here in so many ways. The outdoor tennis courts, for instance, are grass and built to Wimbledon specifications; the Spa, meanwhile, is regularly listed in the top ten in Britain and the top 100 in the world. And if golf at Stoke Park were not sufficient, there are other delightful courses nearby at Burnham Beeches, Beaconsfield, and Denham. South and west London may well offer the highest proportion of good and great courses within a 50-km (30-mile) radius of any capital city.

Golf in & around Stoke Park

Stoke Park Club
Park Road, Stoke Poges
Bucks SL2 4PG
England
Tel: +44 (0)1753 717171
Email: info@stokeparkclub.com
www.stokeparkclub.com/index.php

Sunningdale Golf Club
Ridgemount Road
Sunningdale, Berkshire SL5 9RR
England
Tel: +44 (0)1344 621681
www.sunningdale-golfclub.co.uk

The Wentworth Club
Wentworth Drive, Virginia Water
Surrey GU25 4LS
England
Tel: +44 (0)1344 842201
www.wentworthgolf.co.uk

Les Bordes,
Saint Laurent-Nouan, France

The ancient province of the Orléanais, stretching southwest along the River Loire from Orléans via Beaugency to Blois, is today as peaceful as any region of rural France. But it has not always been so. Its temperate climate and well-stocked larder attracted unwelcome visitors in the Middle Ages, in the form of Huns, Visigoths, and Normans. For centuries to follow, the future of France was decided in battles fought over this land between the English and French, Protestants and Catholics, and more recently between German and Allied forces. Its main thoroughfare is not a road but a river, the Loire. Along its fertile banks are lush pastures, flower gardens, and vineyards, yet it is the infertile soil of the Sologne forests that produces what is reckoned to be the best game to be found in the whole of France, winged-game in particular. Gastronomes of old prized the region's lark and thrush pâtés, rabbit prepared *à la solognote* (in rich wine with onions and mushrooms), Sologne mutton, and the enchantingly scented Orléans quince marmalade.

Kings of France from Charles VII to Henri III preferred the safety of the Loire châteaux to the dangerous political life of Paris, and to this day many Parisian captains of industry have sought solace in this quiet backwater, well away from the tourist tracks yet only a short train ride from the capital city. One such was Baron Marcel Bich, who had made his fortune with Bic pens. He and his friend and business partner, Yoshiaki Sakurai, decided to build the golf course of their dreams in the Sologne landscape a few kilometres from Beaugency. It was a bold venture, for this part of France was not a golfing haven. Golf had always been an upper-class recreation in France, with a few good, but very private, courses around Paris and others along the Channel coast and in the far south. They dated mostly from the early 20th century, and very little had been built in France since then. For Les Bordes the prolific Texan architect Robert von Hagge was engaged to bring his American experience and technique to this pioneering venture.

It must be said that "American experience and technique" do not always guarantee an outstanding course. That Les Bordes is frequently ranked among the finest courses in Europe, ancient or modern, is a testament to von Hagge's outstanding work here. Baron Bich died in 1994, but Yoshiaki Sakurai has continued to maintain Les Bordes as a retreat for the golfer seeking excellent golf in a secluded setting.

The country atmosphere of the Sologne woods is maintained in the accommodation at Les Bordes, with converted farm buildings and cottages providing quiet and comfortable lodgings. The restaurant menu, meanwhile, reflects the hearty produce of the region, with venison, duck, and veal prominent. The Loire valley produces many fine wines, such as Pouilly-Fumé, Sancerre, Vouvray, and Savennières, but for the most part they are white. To accompany the red meat dishes on offer, Les Bordes offers the Baron's own St. Emilion Grand Cru, Château Ferrand.

WATER COMES INTO PLAY ON NO FEWER THAN 12 HOLES AT LES BORDES.

There are a few other golf courses in the area, not least the 36-holes at Ganay owned by the same company, but given the standard set by Les Bordes only a handful of golfers will wish to venture further. Von Hagge made plentiful use of the many ponds on the site, and no fewer than twelve holes are threatened by water. From the back tee there is a considerable carry over water at the 1st, and the green is almost an island completely surrounded by sand. Unusually there is neither water nor sand on the 2nd, but it is narrow and set between trees, a par 5 which dog-legs first left, then right.

Another tight drive follows, possibly the tightest of them all, although the overall length is not troublesome. Big hitters, however, should beware of a little pond hidden in the angle of the dog-leg. Cameras come out on the next hole, the par-3 4th, all carry across water to an angled green. Those who over-club to ensure clearing the water may find their ball nestling in a grassy mound or hollow from which effective escape is no easy matter. Another substantial water-carry is required from the 5th tee, although the good player will be seeking to make the upper portion of the two-level fairway, from which another good strike is necessary to find the green, angled and raised up beyond a bunker.

There is no water on the par-4 6th, but a lengthy bunker lines the right-hand side of the fairway where the long hitter would prefer it did not, and the approach shot is over dead ground to a green eaten into on the right by another sizeable bunker. The par-5 7th is a classic do-or-die hole. Its fairway turns through more than 90-degrees, hugging the shores of a lake as it does so. There is water on both sides of the fairway in the landing zone and, given a successful drive, a decision must then be made about whether to attempt the risky carry, all the way over water, to the green. It is not that much simpler laying up, for the constant curve on the fairway means that the second shot will be hit across the line of the fairway, calling for pinpoint accuracy on length and direction.

OPPOSITE: GRASS BUNKERS ARE A FEATURE OF THE DESIGN OF SEVERAL HOLES AT LES BORDES.

RIGHT: THE 1ST HOLE, NARROW BETWEEN TREES, PLAYED TO A GREEN SURROUNDED BY SAND.

This was, apparently, the Baron's favourite hole. The 8th is another par 3, fairly short, with a compulsory water-carry, but it should not be a cause for concern for the good player. While there is water to the right of the 9th fairway, it really only comes into play for today's biggest hitters. Lesser mortals, after an average drive, should still find the green within range of the second shot, a long, narrow affair with four accompanying bunkers to the sides and rear.

Conveniently, the course returns to the clubhouse at this point. The back nine then sets off with a par 5 running down an avenue of trees. Water does not feature on this hole. Instead, the strategy is dictated by a string of bunkers on the run in to the green. Can they be carried with the second shot? The putting surface is steeply sloped from back to front and overlooks a lake which must be avoided on the 11th. The tees for this hole are set back in trees, from which the water is not readily visible. Anything veering left is heading for trouble. The same is also true of the second shot, the fairway curving left along the shore, the angled green cut off by an inlet of the lake. Yet another lake stretches in front of the next tee, the 12th. While average players will be content just to clear the water, the low-handicapper will want to ensure the drive finishes on the higher part of the fairway, from which it is then possible to carry the several green-front bunkers which protect this shallow putting surface.

Another full carry over water is required on the short 13th, to a heart-shaped green bunkered to the right and through the back of the green. But this is child's play compared with the demands of the 14th, a tricky par 5 of some mischief. It goes without saying that the drive is made out over a portion of the same lake that threatened the 13th. There is another lake to the right, but that should not enter normal play on this hole. Rather more significant is the lake which completely surrounds the island green. There is simply nowhere to bail out on this, arguably the toughest hole on the course.

THE FIRST SHORT HOLE, THE 4TH, DEMANDS PINPOINT ACCURACY.

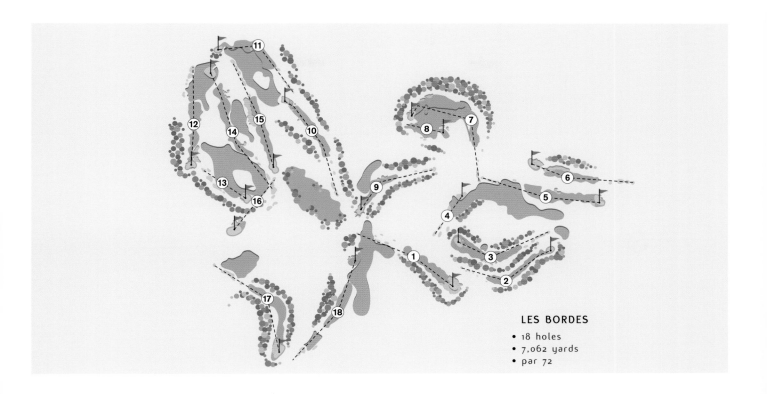

LES BORDES
- 18 holes
- 7,062 yards
- par 72

It comes as something of a relief to find that the 15th is water-free, the drive this time having to avoid a long bunker on the right of the fairway, while the approach is made through humps and bumps to a bunkerless green.

The only dry par 3 follows, uphill to a well-bunkered green and, for those for whom water holds no fear, probably the most demanding of the short holes. Nor does water feature on the 17th, a long par 4 dog-legged to the right. Good distance off the tee is an asset here, opening up the green to view and allowing an approach down the length of the angled green, rather than across its generous accompanying bunker to the narrowest part of the putting surface. Water returns with a vengeance on the final hole. First it must be cleared from the tee. Then, and rather more threateningly, it must be carried on the long approach to the sloping green. As if to add injury to insult the lake also hugs the right side of the green and the contours of the putting surface are complex and deceptive.

Contact:

Les Bordes
41220 Saint-Laurent-Nouan
France
Tel: +33 (0) 450 26 85 00
Email: info@lesbordes.com
www.lesbordes.com

Royal Parc Evian, France

Evian-les-Bains is one of the leading spas in Europe, occupying a good vantage point on the south shore of Lake Geneva. The town was rebuilt in its present form in 1865 by Baron de Blonay, and there is something about the ornate public buildings which continues to lend an old-fashioned feel to it, reminding many Britons of Harrogate and Buxton, Malvern and Bath. Now drunk all over the world, Evian water is one of the most widely exported of French table waters, and is said to work wonders for arthritis and miracles for the kidneys! Evian has everything a fashionable resort should have, including a casino, conference halls, golf, sailing, a concert hall, and sophisticated night life. The little town is full to the brim with hotels and restaurants, but the grandest place to stay is undoubtedly the Hôtel Royal.

The hotel was built as a key part of an impressive scheme drawn up in 1904 by Pierre Girod, son of the founder of the Société des Eaux Minérales d'Evian, and intended to welcome Edward VII of England. At that time Evian was perceived to be lagging behind other European watering holes, and it was felt that its facilities needed to be greatly upgraded and enlarged if it was to attract the English-speaking wealthy and aristocratic classes to spend their summers in the town. Naturally a golf course was required, and the task of designing it fell to Willie Park Jr, who had recently completed the first course at Sunningdale which had opened to great critical acclaim. His course at Evian was on a smaller scale, being only 9 holes, but it attracted the right clientele, early visitors including the Baron de Neuflize, the Vicomte de Sallmard, the Duc de Nemours, Comte de Talleyrand, Prince Takamatsu of Japan, the Marquis de Bretteville, and a Doctor Rothschild from California. Arnaud Massy, who had won the Open Championship at Hoylake in 1907, became the club's Professional in 1909. A further 9 holes were added in 1924 and the course was redesigned twice more, first in 1976 and then again between 1988 and 1990. The American course architect Cabell Robinson was responsible for this last rebuild, his first

design in Europe, bringing the course right up to date as far as hosting the Evian Masters is concerned. This annual tournament brings together the top lady professionals of the world, and is co-sanctioned by the American (LPGA) and European tours. World No. 1 and two-time Evian Masters winner Annika Sorenstam once observed, "I wouldn't miss this tournament for anything. It's always had a very special place in my heart".

Although set on high ground overlooking Lake Geneva and with the French Alps as a dramatic backcloth, the course is not exhaustingly hilly and is easily walked. The distant views are pleasing and change constantly, while nearer at hand century-old trees frame many fairways, although not to the point of excess. At a little under 6,600 yards from the tips, with a par of 72, the course is a good length for social golf, with plenty of variety and enough challenge to keep the low-handicappers on their toes, yet reasonably forgiving for the less competitive player. The 1st hole, however, is not a gentle introduction, with a sloping fairway which accentuates the merest trace of early slice and an angled green which demands an approach played from the left of the fairway.

A POND GUARDS THE 18TH GREEN (LEFT), WHILE FROM THE BACK TEE THE DRIVE IS MADE OVER ANOTHER POND TO FIND THE 1ST FAIRWAY (FOREGROUND).

THE HÔTEL ERMITAGE, BUILT IN THE STYLE
OF A SAVOYARD CHALET.

At 514 yards, the par-5 2nd is certainly within reach of two shots to a good player, as long as a line of bunkers eating into the fairway short of the green is cleared comfortably. A longish par 3 and a comparatively simple short par 5 follow, leading to the agreeably strategic 5th, a par 4 of 414 yards on which a large chestnut tree cuts out the approach shots of those who carelessly allow their drive to slip too far to the right. The 6th winds back up the hill in parallel, its green raised, sloping, and guarded by bunkers. Good placement of the drive is again important on the 7th, the longest two-shot hole on the course at 423 yards. Another mid-length par 4 is encountered at the 8th, while from the back tee the 9th is stern, a par 3 of 238 yards. The longest par 3 then gives way to the

longest hole on the course, the 548-yard 10th, a demanding hole because the green is set up on two levels behind a stream. From any distance the approach to it is testing, and even for the longest hitter, who might expect to get home in two, it is a decision not to be undertaken lightly. The problem is that good length from the tee requires a very sure technique, with out-of-bounds on the right and the fairway sloping down to thick rough on the left. At 306 yards the 11th is a very short par 4, but the green is hidden round a corner, behind trees, and only an approach played from the left of the fairway stands much chance of finding it. It is followed by a very short par 3, only 113 yards long, which plays downhill to the green, requiring a delicately judged tee shot to find the putting surface.

In front of the green on the par-5 13th, the stream which governed play on the 10th makes a reappearance. This time, however, the hole is 481 yards long. The green is therefore in reach of two shots to many more players, and the temptation to go for broke is all the greater. Straight driving is again required on the narrow 420-yard 14th, with trees lining the fairway on the right and the out-of-bounds practice ground on the left. The short 15th enjoys a wonderful panorama over Lake Geneva. From here the finish is not arduous — two short par 4s either side of the 421-yard 17th — and precision play is of greater value than outright strength.

After the round, it is time to relax with a glass of one of the light, dry wines of

GLORIOUS VIEWS ABOUND AT EVIAN'S 15TH HOLE.

THE SAVOYARD CHALET THEME IS CARRIED THROUGH INTO THE COURSE BUILDINGS AT EVIAN.

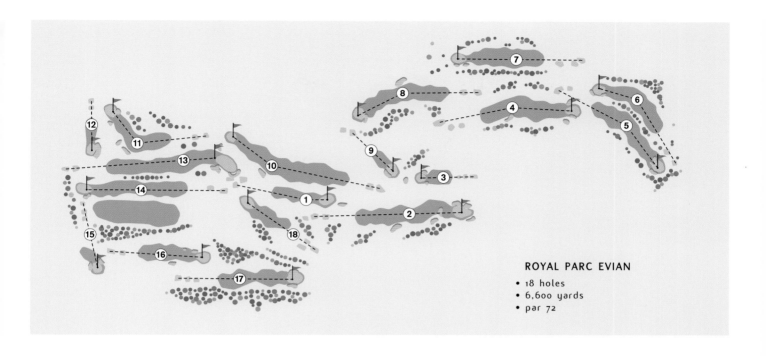

ROYAL PARC EVIAN
- 18 holes
- 6,600 yards
- par 72

Savoie — Apremont, Crépy, Seyssel, or Roussette, perhaps — to accompany a typical regional dish, served in the mountain chalet-style clubhouse. Eating on a rather grander scale can be found in any one of the nine restaurants at Royal Parc Evian, each with its own cuisine and menu. The contestants in the Evian Masters generally stay at the 91-room Hôtel Ermitage, a very comfortable country house in the style of a Savoyard chalet. Those who want the ultimate in sumptuousness should opt for the Hôtel Royal, a uniquely opulent grand hotel retaining the style and décor chosen for Edward VII's visit.

Golfing activities run from February to November, although the best period on the course is May to September. During the other months winter sports take precedence, with alpine, cross-country, powder, and glacier skiing, snowboarding, dog-sledding and heliskiing leading the way. Other sports featured at Royal Parc Evian are tennis, archery, climbing, mountain-biking, potholing, riding, rafting, canoeing, waterskiing, sailing, hot-air ballooning, paragliding, and free-fall parachuting. With Evian's reputation as a health-giving spa, it goes without saying that Royal Parc's raft of relaxation and re-energizing facilities is second to none. And if there is still a little cash left in the wallet, the gaming tables, slot machines, nightclub, bars, and restaurants of the Casino are always there to solve that problem.

Contact:

Royal Parc Evian
74500 Evian-les-Bains
France
Tel: +33 (0)450 26 85 00
Email: reservation@royalparcevian.com
www.royalparcevian.com

Adare Manor & Southern Ireland

Over the last quarter of a century there has been nothing short of a golfing boom in Ireland. New courses have sprung up at an astonishing rate, some of them among Europe's finest, and many old courses once known only to locals and a few aficionados now boast international memberships and fame throughout the whole of the golfing world. Ireland's prosperity has grown dramatically over the same period, and it is now richly endowed with outstanding hotels and restaurants. Unfortunately it is no longer an inexpensive country, but there is no denying the quality of good living and golf to be found in the Republic.

Historically, Ireland was a land of big country estates, but some foundered in times of poverty, such as the potato famine; others were abandoned when the Republic separated from British rule in 1922; and others simply proved too expensive to maintain in modern times. Some of these are now country house hotels, and of these Adare Manor is one of the most prominent. Curiously, it was built to give the Second Earl of Dunraven something to do! As he suffered from gout and could not take part in the usual country pursuits of the landed classes, his wife put him in charge of the building's construction. He did not live long enough to see its completion, but the house remained in the family until 1982. The Thomas F. Kane family of Florida acquired the estate in 1987 and began the task of restoring and converting it into a top-class resort.

With its towers and turrets reflected in the waters of the River Maigue, Adare Manor is reminiscent in many ways of a Loire château, and there is more than a touch of French cuisine to the exquisite fare served in the Oakroom Fine Dining Restaurant. Wisely, the majority of ingredients are sourced locally, for Ireland is renowned for the quality of its produce, and not least for the excellent fish and shellfish caught in the Atlantic waters off its west coast. Guests at Adare Manor can catch their own salmon and brown trout in the grounds, and gillies, fishing tackle, and all necessary permits are available at the Manor. Ireland is also famed for its horses, and equestrian pursuits are on a grand scale here. Hunting with three local packs is available from the beginning of November to the end of February. Cross-country riding and trekking are also offered, as are dressage and show jumping. For those who fancy a flutter on the horses, Limerick race course is the newest in Ireland, and the first to be built in over fifty years. Adare is possibly the prettiest village in Ireland, with no end of buildings and places of historic interest within easy reach.

ARNOLD PALMER MADE SPECTACULAR USE OF THESE DUNES
ON THE BACK NINE AT TRALEE ON IRELAND'S ATLANTIC COAST.

THE 15TH ON THE OLD COURSE AT BALLYBUNION, ONE OF IRELAND'S GREATEST PAR 3S.

Of the other courses in the region, Old Head is controversial. Laid out on a clifftop promontory projecting 3 km (2 miles) into the Atlantic, in good weather this is one of the most stunning golfing places on earth. When the wind blows, however, it does so seriously, and with one of the highest green fees in Europe this is not a course to walk off after only a few holes! Killarney was begun by Lord Castlerosse, a man with an ebullient personality every bit as large as his girth. With the help of Sir Guy Campbell and Henry Longhurst, he laid out one of Ireland's prettiest courses on the shores of Lough Leane, in the shadow of Macgillicuddy's Reeks. Sadly, it is no longer possible to play the course in its original configuration as it was split in two when further holes were added, and more recently an additional 18 holes were constructed to make a total of 54. The Irish Open was played here in 1991 and 1992, when Nick Faldo triumphed. Henry Longhurst summed it up in typically picturesque fashion: "What a lovely place to die!"

However, it is for golf that we have come to Adare Manor, for not only does it have its own Robert Trent Jones course, but it is also lies within relatively easy reach of Ballybunion, Ceann Sibeal, Dooks, Doonbeg, Killarney, Lahinch, Old Head, Tralee and Waterville: a star-studded list for sure. Adare Manor's course is a big one, 7,138 yards from the championship tees; a lake enters play on the front nine and the back nine wander through tree-lined avenues. Many of the Trent Jones hallmarks are present, especially the vast clover-leaf bunkers, and the conditioning of the course is exemplary. It should be noted that while Adare Manor is the name of the house and resort, the name of its golf course is plain Adare (Adare Manor confusingly being the name of another club and course in the village, and a rather charming one at that).

Ceann Sibeal is the most westerly course in Europe, wild and remote on the Dingle Peninsula, a reminder of what golf was like in 1924 when it was founded. Dooks is an even older club, dating back to 1889, and again it is a traditional links. On the drive to either club from Adare you will pass through Tralee. Although this too is an old club (1896), Tralee moved to a new course beyond Ardfert in 1984, laid out by Arnold Palmer.

TOM FAZIO HAS MADE RECENT AMENDMENTS TO WATERVILLE'S LINKS COURSE, TO TAKE EVEN GREATER ADVANTAGE OF ITS NATURAL DUNESLAND.

THE PAR-3 FINAL HOLE ON THE HANDSOME MAHONEY'S POINT COURSE AT KILLARNEY.

A dramatic spot on tumbling dunes above the pounding Atlantic breakers, this was once the favourite haunt of pirates and later featured as one of the locations used in the film *Ryan's Daughter*. In a wind it can become a monster. Remaining in County Kerry, there are two majestic links courses at Ballybunion. Neither should be missed. There are some who find Ballybunion's Cashen Course just too difficult. It was designed by Robert Trent Jones, who was not going to pass up on the offer of one of the most promising stretches of duneland imaginable. He took advantage of the varied topography to create a really

challenging links, with greens clinging to mountainous dunes, fairways squeezed through them, and tees assembled like gun platforms. Cashen is hard, but it is a once in a lifetime experience. The Old Course at Ballybunion is one of the world's greatest. It is laid out over, through, round, and alongside more of these amazing dunes, in such a way that there is probably no better test of the approach shot in golf.

To the north of Adare, two links courses in County Clare in particular deserve a mention: Doonbeg and Lahinch. The work of the Australian golfer Greg Norman, Doonbeg is already highly acclaimed.

Given some spectacular dunes through which to route the course, Norman has not been afraid of using them. Lahinch is often described as the Irish St. Andrews. It has had a first-rate links course since 1892, when Old Tom Morris laid it out. Since then several other architects have had a hand in its evolution, principally Alister Mackenzie, but the recent (1999) restoration by Martin Hawtree has been particularly noteworthy, especially for his re-opening of some of the most engaging duneland. After Hawtree's changes, the course has raced up to the top of the ranking charts so beloved by today's golf magazines.

Finally, returning south to County Kerry, Waterville is an old club dating back to 1889, founded by men working on the first trans-Atlantic cable which came ashore here. It was a modest 9-hole course which fell out of use, along with the cable, during the 1950s. An Irish-American, John Mulcahy recognized the potential of the place, and engaged the shy Irishman Eddie Hackett to lay out the course of his dreams, with input also from Claude Harmon, a past Masters champion. With its archetypal dunes and superb situation, set on a headland almost surrounded by the sea against a sublime mountain backdrop, it has been one of the gems of Irish links golf ever since. Interestingly, the club recently brought the very well-known American architect Tom Fazio over to make a number of revisions, principally in order to make rather more of the dunes and to eliminate the odd dull spot early on in the round. Now Waterville will be even more worthy of Sam Snead's description of it as "one of the golfing wonders of the world".

WATERVILLE GOLF LINKS COURSE

- 18 holes
- 7,225 yards
- par 72

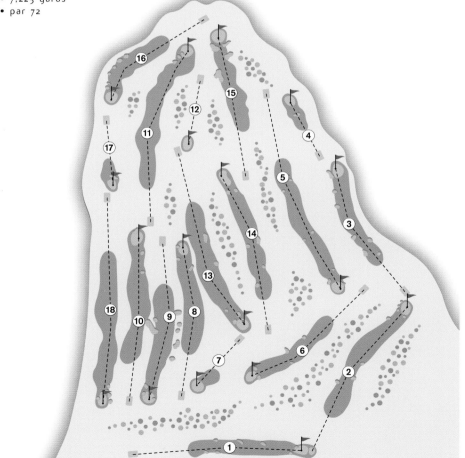

Golf in & around Southern Ireland

Adare Manor Hotel and Golf Resort
Adare, Co. Limerick
Ireland
Tel: +353 (0)61 396566
Toll Free (USA and Canada): 1 800 462 3273
Freephone (UK): 0800 904 7523
Email: reservations@adaremanor.com
www.adaremanor.ie

Ballybunion Golf Course
Ballybunion, Co. Kerry
Ireland
Tel: +353 (0)68 27146
Email: bbgolfc@iol.ie
www.ballybuniongolfclub.iel

Lahinch Golf Club
Lahinch. Co. Clare
Ireland
Tel: +353 (0)65 7081003
Email: info@lahinchgolf.com
www.lahinchgolf.com

Waterville Golf Links
Waterville, Co. Kerry
Ireland
Tel: +353 (0)66 9474102
Email: wvgolf@iol.ie
www.watervillegolflinks.ie

Killarney Golf and Fishing Club
Killarney, Co. Kerry
Ireland
Tel: +353 (0)64 31024
Email: reservations@killarney-golf.com
www.killarney-golf.com

Cabo del Sol, Mexico

Baja California is a long, thin peninsula, stretching south for hundreds of miles from the northernmost tip of Mexico into the Pacific Ocean, and separated from the rest of Mexico by the Sea of Cortés. It is an extraordinary place, a mixture of beautiful deserts, mountains, pine forests, cacti (of course), and mile upon mile of unspoiled coastline. While it is remote enough from the mainland for most Mexicans to think of it as another country, it is becoming increasingly popular with visitors from the northern United States and Canada, especially during the winter months when breezes off the Pacific Ocean give the region a warm, Mediterranean-like climate. Nor are humans the only northern visitors at this time of year. In one of the largest mammal migrations of all, huge numbers of grey whale make a 16,000-kilometre (10,000-mile) round trip from their Arctic feeding grounds to the sheltered bays of Baja California to breed. Whale-watching trips have become a major tourist industry in this part of Mexico.

Right on the southern tip of Baja California are Los Cabos, two towns about 32 km (20 miles) apart which were originally centres for deep-sea fishing, most notably marlin. Cabo San Lucas, to the west, is a modern tourist town with a huge marina, lively nightlife, and a vast array of restaurants offering a wide range of cooking styles. It is also where the Pacific Ocean meets the Sea of Cortés, at a promontory plunging into the ocean and eroded into a dramatic arch known as El Arco. Pelicans spread their wings in the sun on the rocky islands offshore, before making another foray to feed on the brightly coloured fish that are so abundant in these waters.

To the east is San José del Cabo, founded by a Jesuit priest, Nicholas Tamaral, in the early 1730s. Spanish ships had been coming here for a century or more to take on fresh water after the arduous journey across the Pacific from the Philippines. Pirate raids and the less than friendly welcome afforded them by local people meant that there had been a Spanish military presence in the region during the 1720s. Tamaral, however, established a mission. When he was killed in 1734, the Spanish set up a Presidio where they remained until the mid-19th century. For this reason many old buildings have survived, and San José del Cabo remains a quiet town of art galleries, restaurants, and boutiques, very different in atmosphere from the fiesta-like Cabo San Lucas.

Between the two towns lies an area known as the Corridor, which is rapidly becoming a focus for resort development. This is hardly surprising, for the average daytime temperature throughout the year is 25°C (78°F), the region basks in 350 sunny days a year, and more than 20 flights arrive each day from the USA. Inevitably there is golf, with Cabo del Sol in particular offering two courses, one designed by Jack Nicklaus and the other by Tom Weiskopf, with two more in the pipeline. Vying with golf as the most popular sport here, however, must be deep-sea fishing. Blue and black marlin are fished from June to December, striped marlin all year round, and sailfish from April to October. Swordfish are also a popular catch. Plentiful fish ensure vibrant birdlife — 150 different species of bird make their home in the estuary at San José del Cabo. Naturalists also enjoy the diverse habitats inland in the canyons and arroyos, mountains and desert. These also make for good mountain-biking, 4 x 4 driving, and excursions on horseback. Riding on the beach is popular, naturally, and water sports include surfing, scuba diving, parasailing, windsurfing, and just plain sailing.

THE 5TH AND 6TH GREENS ON THE OCEAN COURSE AT CABO DEL SOL.

THE WONDERFULLY-SITED 18TH GREEN OF THE OCEAN COURSE.

Cabo del Sol offers two complementary places to stay: the Sheraton Hacienda del Mar and Fiesta Americana Grand. Built in the style of a traditional Spanish hacienda, Hacienda del Mar boasts 270 guest rooms, ranging from imposing suites to deluxe rooms, and all with private balconies overlooking the sea, gardens, or golf course. Girasoles de la Hacienda is their traditional Mexican restaurant, Pitahayas a wonderfully located beachside restaurant offering Pacific rim cuisine, Los Tomates serves international cuisine, and the D'Cortez grill features prime meat cuts and seafood cooked on a wood grill.

The almost equally large Fiesta Americana Grand has 267 rooms, each with a private balcony overlooking the Sea of Cortés,

and again ranging from deluxe rooms to a variety of suites. Viña del Mar is the international restaurant here, while El Rosato specialises in seafood and northern Italian cuisine. Choosing between the two hotels is a tricky proposition!

Jack Nicklaus and his team were given an inspiring stretch of coastline alongside which to lay out the first course at Cabo del Sol, the Ocean Course. Cleverly, they arranged the routing so that parts of both 9-hole loops touch the Pacific, giving several high spots during the round and leading to a magnificent finish. The ocean is visible from most parts of the course, and is very much a factor in the play of the coastal holes. Starting off inland, however, the first two holes climb towards

the Tiburon arroyo, both curving to the right and quite long from the back tees. A short par 4, the 3rd, and another par 5 begin the descent towards the ocean, which is reached on the 5th green. This is a very strong hole, 458 yards from the back, on which the good player is encouraged to risk cutting the corner of the dog-leg in order to get a better angle of approach to the beach-front green. That Nicklaus did not resort to formulaic design is obvious from the next two holes, back-to-back par 3s. On paper this might look like a weakness, but in fact it is an inspired use of natural resources to give two spectacular holes. Both involve tee-shots played over the ocean, the 6th to a green sitting on a granite outcrop, the 7th to a green set on a large sand dune.

CABO DEL SOL'S PAR-3 17TH.

THE 16TH GREEN OF CABO DEL SOL'S OCEAN COURSE WITH THE 17TH GREEN BEHIND.

THE OCEAN COURSE
- 18 holes
- 7,103 yards
- par 72

Contact:

For general resort info and golf tee time reservations see: www.cabodelsol.com

Sheraton Hacienda del Mar
Tel: +52 624 145 8000
(from USA) 1 (888) 672 7137
Fax: +52 624 145 8002
Email:
information@sheratonhaciendadelmar.com

Fiesta Americana Grand
Tel: +52 624 145-6200
(from USA) 1 (800) FIESTA1
Fax: +52 624 145-6201
Email: reserv@fiestaamericana.com.mx

From the 15th hole the finish is superb. The setting and astute bunkering of the 15th make it an enjoyable par 5, not so difficult that the marvellous views cannot be appreciated. Continuing the journey to the water's edge, the 16th is a mid-length two-shot hole on which the excitement of floating the approach shot against the backdrop of the ocean is pure magic. Like the 6th and 7th, the 17th is a short hole played across the Pacific to the green. Where the ocean was on the left of the earlier holes, now it is on the right. It is not over-long, but the penalty for missing this picture-postcard green is all too obvious. The 18th is a splendidly natural hole, hugging the beach and the ocean all the way from tee to green, and curving in a gentle arc as it does so. There is room for the timid golfer to play safely away from the water, but the player who is prepared to flirt with the ocean down the right — and who does so successfully — can appreciably shorten the second shot to the green perched right on the edge of the ocean.

Tom Weiskopf's Desert Course opened in 2002. As its name implies, it is laid out in dramatic inland country, although there are wide seascapes visible from most parts of the course. Like the Ocean Course it is long from the back tees (7,097 yards), but there are multiple tees to suit the games of all handicap ranges. Despite the overall length there is considerable variety to hole lengths, with two monster par 5s (626-yard 3rd and 592-yard 12th), par 3s from 170 to 234 yards, and two-shot holes from 329 to 480 yards. Overall, the Desert and Ocean Courses between them make an engagingly contrasting pair of courses with the convenience of being in one resort. Wait until there are four!

Kauri Cliffs and Cape Kidnappers, New Zealand

There are more golf courses per thousand of the population in New Zealand than in any other country. Statistically, then, New Zealand's players live in a golfing paradise. In reality, however, there are not too many top-rank courses for them to play. Paraparaumu Beach, Christchurch, and Titirangi had the field pretty much to themselves for many years, and tournament golf rotated between these three and Auckland's course at Belmont, a good course but not quite in the same league. The New Zealand government's Tourist Hotel Corporation recognized this lack of provision, and in 1970 opened the Wairakei International Golf Course. This was ground-breaking for New Zealand, in that it played to 7,000 yards from the back tees and was not near a centre of population. It was laid out amid the forests and streams of the Lake Taupo region, in which golf is frequently punctuated by the belching of sulphurous clouds from the geothermal fields at nearby Karapiti and Rogue. A fine course, it was recognized as such in 1996 when *Golf Digest* voted it the 17th best public course in the world outside America.

Courses of a similar standing did not follow rapidly, but in the 21st century a number of resorts are now able to boast good all-round facilities in terms of accommodation, other activities, and golf. Among these are Terrace Downs, Clearwater Resort and Millbrook in the South Island, and Gulf Harbour and Formosa Country Club in the North Island. Two courses which stand out for their incomparable settings and great golfing challenges, however, are Cape Kidnappers and Kauri Cliffs. Although they are both on North Island they are quite some distance apart and better treated as separate entities.

Cape Kidnappers is set on spectacular cliffs overlooking the sea to the south of Hawke's Bay on the east coast, one of New Zealand's premier wine-growing districts. The vines were originally planted by French missionaries to make their communion wine, and French varieties predominate to this day, producing full-bodied Cabernet Sauvignon, Merlot, Chardonnay, and Sauvignon wines. Captain James Cook was almost certainly the first European to visit Hawke's Bay, arriving in 1769. He and his crew then sailed south in the *Endeavour* and encountered some traders in canoes. As the traders left the ship and began paddling back to shore, the sailors noticed that they had taken with them a Tahitian boy from the *Endeavour*. Shots were fired and several Maoris were killed, together with the unfortunate boy, who was trying to swim back to his ship. As a result of this incident, Cook gave the name Cape Kidnappers to the spot where the golf course stands today. But a far older legend is attached to this part of the North Island. Maui-tikitiki-a-Taranga, a mythical figure of Maori folklore, was fishing one day when he suddenly revealed magical powers. After chanting a prayer, he spread blood onto a magic jawbone and with it landed a gigantic fish, Te-Ika-a-Maui, the Fish of Maui. When he had gone, his companions took chunks out of the fish, which explains why the North Island is the shape it is, why its coastline is so jagged, and why Hawke's Bay is in the shape of that magic jawbone.

KAURI CLIFFS. IT IS DIFFICULT TO CONCENTRATE ON GOLF WHEN THE SURROUNDING SCENERY IS SO SPECTACULAR.

THE GREEN OF THE SHORT PAR-4 3RD AT KAURI CLIFFS UNDULATES SIGNIFICANTLY.

Tom Doak, one of the most inspired architects in golf today, was commissioned to lay out the Cape Kidnappers course. It is a remarkable place, with ridges following the lines of the cliffs as they run in parallel lines to the point where they make an abrupt halt, falling sheer to the waves 120 m (400 ft) below. Doak routed the course so that several times the golfer must play to a green which appears to be at the very end of the earth. Overshoot one of these greens and, according to Doak, it takes a full ten seconds for the ball to career down into the surf. It is not a links course but it certainly plays fast and firm, and if there is any wind to be found it will be up here. Accommodation is not provided at the golf course, but there are a number of excellent hotels in the Hawke's Bay area, such as the Cellar Master's Cottage at Craggy Range Winery or Green Hill the Lodge, an opulent country house in a remarkable colonial style, again in the heart of wine country.

Kauri Cliffs is much further north on North Island, and by far the most scenic route from Cape Kidnappers would be by helicopter, which is perfectly feasible. Alternatively, there are flights from Auckland to Kerikeri airport, which is only a short drive from the resort. Kauri Cliffs has its own accommodation, the very smart Lodge, with 22 comfortable guest suites located in 11 cottages. The setting alone is special, overlooking the cliffs and miles and miles of open sea, but then so is everything here. Dinner is formal, and like all the cooking here makes imaginative use of the fine local ingredients: vegetables and fruits, meat, and seafood. Three private beaches are available for the use of guests, and picnic hampers are a speciality of the kitchen. Hunting for wild boar, pheasant, waterfowl or even possum is popular, as are deep-sea fishing, diving, snorkelling, and boating in almost any shape or form. Tours of the area's unique attractions, historical and natural, are many and varied.

The golf course was designed by David Harman, who has constructed courses for Jack Nicklaus, Pete Dye, Tom Fazio, and Arnold Palmer. One of the great merits of a location such as this is that it offers many possibilities for wonderfully sited greens. As early as the 1st, a fairly straightforward par 4, the green is set at the end of a gentle descent with a big drop-off to the side and beyond. Doak's "end of the earth" description comes to mind. There is a similar situation on the 2nd, and already the course is asking a good deal of the player's nerve and resolve on the approach shot. Trees complicate the approach to the short par-4 3rd, turning inland, before the par-5 4th heads off towards the sea, once again enjoying marvellous seascapes from its elevated fairway. Yet again its green is not one to overshoot. The first short hole is all carry across rough ground and bunkers, although there is an option of playing to fairway left of the green for those whose confidence fails them. Climbing towards the skyline, the 6th continues the journey towards the sea.

THE 13TH AND 14TH HOLES AT KAURI CLIFFS.

THE 7TH, CAVALLI, PLAYS ACROSS THE CLIFFS IN THE FOREGROUND WITH THE PAR-5 8TH STRETCHING BEYOND.

Kauri Cliffs and Cape Kidnappers, New Zealand

KAURI CLIFFS COURSE

- 18 holes
- 7,119 yards
- par 72

Contact:

The Lodge at Kauri Cliffs
Matauri Bay Road
Matauri Bay
Northland
New Zealand
Tel: +64 9 407 0010
Email: info@kauricliffs.com
www.kauricliffs.com

Cape Kidnappers
448 Clifton Road
Te Awanga
Hawke's Bay
New Zealand
Tel (Golf Shop): +64 6 875 1900
Email: proshop@capekidnappers.com
www.capekidnappers.com

It is followed by the heart-stopping 220-yard 7th. There is no ducking the challenge with a formidable carry over an abyss, the cliffs tumbling towards the sea on the right, forming a magnificent backdrop. A cleverly bunkered par 5 and an uphill two-shot hole bring play back to the Lodge.

The back nine set off along a valley with a stream and marshy land awaiting inaccurate shots, before the 13th takes play onto higher ground. On the long par-3 14th the views are superb, with the sea as an expansive background and the green overlooking the Cavalli Islands. With bunkers to the right and a steep drop to the left, this is not a green to miss. Left is not the side to be on the 15th, either, with cliffs plunging steeply down only just off the fairway's edge, and again the sensation is very much of playing to the ends of the earth. Continuing this spectacular journey along the cliffs, the short par-4 16th curves gently downhill to the left towards the sea. There is an invitation to try to drive the green, with plentiful bunkers and steep drops to penalize those whose execution falls short of perfection. The last of this sequence of cliff-top holes, the 17th, is a strong par 4 falling towards yet another land's end green, while, inevitably, the last hole climbs back steadily towards the Lodge.

Hotel Quinta do Lago,
Almancil, Algarve, Portugal

Portugal, one of Europe's oldest nations, is now one of Europe's premier golf destinations. Thousands of golfers flock to its sun-drenched courses, particularly during the winter months in order to escape the cold and darkness of northern Europe. It is one of the great success stories of contemporary golf tourism. British wine exporters established a club in Oporto in the 1890s, but the game was greeted with little enthusiasm among the Portuguese themselves, and by the outbreak of the Second World War there were only seven courses scattered through Portugal, Madeira, and the Azores.

It was Henry Cotton's 1966 championship course at Penina which demonstrated the golfing potential of Portugal in general and the Algarve in particular, and since then a host of fine courses have been constructed, with many more in the pipeline. They benefit from modern construction techniques, using grass strains suited to the climate, and are not only well drained and properly irrigated, but also, for the most part, well designed, beautifully conditioned, and expertly managed. The extensive Quinta do Lago (farm by the lake) estate has four 18-hole top-class golf courses of its own, with a further eight within easy reach. It makes a perfect location for a golf-oriented holiday or break.

Quinta do Lago offers all the creature comforts and leisure activities one might expect of a top flight resort, with a health club, swimming pools, tennis, water sports, scuba diving, fishing, and riding, plus two fine restaurants, one serving Italian cuisine and the other a mixture of Portuguese and international styles.

And the Algarve itself is a fascinating region well worth exploring, full of little villages with cobbled streets and buildings clearly influenced by North African architecture. It is also packed with restaurants serving fascinating local dishes, many of them making use of the abundant fish found in its Atlantic waters, such as freshly grilled sardines or swordfish steaks, clams steamed with sausages, ham and garlic, and the famous *bacalhau* (salt cod). Though improving, the local wines are not yet at the level of those from further north, which currently offer some of the best value in Europe for quality wines: from the Douro River, Dão, Bairrada, Estremadura, and Ribatejo. Many wines from the Alentejo region, just north of the Algarve, are now making great strides and should be easily available. Proper *vinho verde* is a revelation to drinkers used to the pappy, slightly sweet concoction all too frequently found in the export market. The real thing is dry, slightly prickly, and wonderfully thirst-quenching.

FOUR 18-HOLE COURSES LIE WITHIN THE BOUNDARIES
OF THE QUINTA DO LAGO ESTATE.

Some 800 hectares (2,000 acres) of rolling, sandy land make up the Quinta do Lago estate. True, there is housing development within it, not to mention the hotel and golf courses, but it is maintained as a vast nature reserve with abundant flora and fauna. The umbrella pines that flourish here provide shelter, while the quiet waters and marshlands of the Ria Formosa estuary are a protected haven for birdlife.

Although the original Quinta do Lago course is the jewel in the resort's crown, and has hosted eight Portuguese Opens on the European Tour, the hotel will also book rounds for visitors at many other courses, including Pinheiros Altos, Vila Sol, and the several Vilamoura courses. All can be recommended for the variety and interest of their challenges. Vilamoura Old, meanwhile, is one of the distinguished and venerable gentlemen of the Algarve, a lovely Frank Pennink course of 1969 which has maintained its reputation as a brilliant design, despite the gauntlets thrown down by the many newer pretenders. It was substantially renovated in 2003.

The oldest course on the estate was the original Vale de Lobo (valley of the wolf), laid out by Sir Henry Cotton in 1968. Other holes were later added, and when the courses came under new ownership in 1987 they were split into a new configuration mixing holes from each to make what are now called the Royal and Ocean Courses.

THE 7TH HOLE AT SAN LORENZO SKIRTS THE NATURE RESERVE OF THE RIA FORMOSA.

The 16th hole of the Royal Course is one of the most photographed holes in the world, a 224-yard carry across deep gullies of red ochre crumbling onto the beach and into the sea. It must be said, though, that however good the course may be (also a Portuguese Open venue), housing development has made itself very conspicuous in recent years. There is something more attractive, though less spectacular, about the Ocean Course, especially as it drops down through the pines to the 15th green beside the beach.

Quinta do Lago also has two courses that have been played in various configurations over the years. Happily the 18 championship holes have been retained as the Quinta do Lago South Course, while the other 18, once called Ria Formosa, have now been renamed Quinta do Lago North. The North Course is certainly not to be sniffed at, and is very attractive in the way it weaves through stands of umbrella pines and over gently undulating ground along an out-and-back routing of the type that was so common in the early days of golf. The South Course is similarly appealing, but there is more water in play and at one end the course wanders down to the edge of the Ria Formosa reserve. This was the first course in Portugal to be designed by an American, William Mitchell.

In 1988 another American, Joseph Lee (assisted by Rocky Roquemore), built San Lorenzo, which quickly established itself among the top ten courses in continental Europe. The course is on the estate, close to the hotel, and although it is not officially part of the resort it is possible to book tee times at San Lorenzo through the hotel and it is worth making every effort to play it, for it is magical. It might be wondered how a private course hosting no professional tournaments and keeping itself very much to itself manages consistently to attract the attentions of the ranking panels who rate courses for the golfing press. Well, it simply oozes quality, presents an excellent all-round test of the game, is immaculately prepared, and is stunningly beautiful. Simple, really!

What makes San Lorenzo stand out from the other Portuguese courses, good though so many of them are, is its

THE MUCH-PHOTOGRAPHED PAR-3 15TH ON QUINTA DO LAGO SOUTH COURSE.

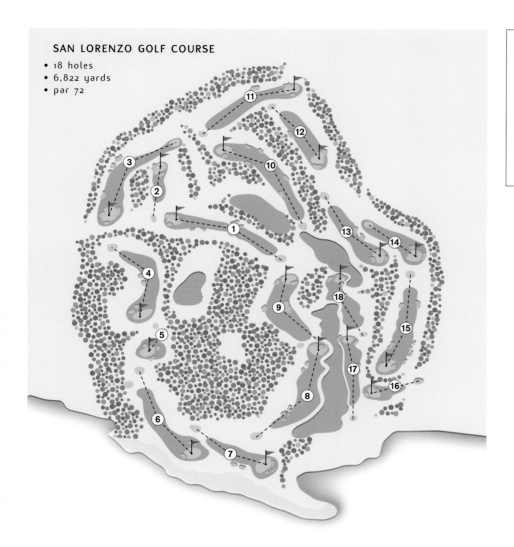

SAN LORENZO GOLF COURSE

- 18 holes
- 6,822 yards
- par 72

Contact:

Hotel Quinta do Lago
Almancil
Algarve
8135-024
Portugal
Tel: +351 289 350 350
Email: info@quintadolagohotel.com
www.hotelquintadolago.com

possession of two stretches of holes of rare beauty. The first sequence comes on the front nine when suddenly the par-3 5th breaks out from the trees, a short hole played across a gully to a green backed by the Atlantic Ocean. Then the 6th and 7th both hug the Ria Formosa, the merest hint of fade enough to find its waters, and trouble aplenty in the pines and scrubby dunes on the left. Turning inland, along the side of a lagoon, comes the par-5 8th, and at 574 yards, this is a hole on which the golfer would prefer not to have to hold back. Lee kept his other stunning holes for the finish, running up the opposite bank of the lagoon from the 8th. On the 17th the fairway slopes towards its waters, bunkers assisting the process, and the pitch is made over the water to a small green.

Then the drive at the 18th is made alongside the lagoon, again bordering the left side of the fairway. There is plenty of room on the right, but the further right the drive is hit, the longer will be the approach shot and the more water, this time on the right, will have to be carried to reach the green. It is a great strategic hole and a brilliant finish to an inspiring course.

The Gleneagles Hotel,
Perthshire, Scotland

Gleneagles was the brainchild of one Donald Matheson, General Manager of the Caledonian Railway Company. Matheson believed that, if he could provide the public with a first-class hotel boasting first-class amenities, a "Palace in the Glens", he would be able to persuade royalty, nobility, and the wealthy to travel on his railway line. Work was soon interrupted by the First World War, however, and it was not until 1924 that Matheson's "Riviera in the Highlands" was officially opened. By then the Caledonian Railway had been amalgamated into the London Midland and Scottish Railway, a much larger company with direct services to Scotland from London, the Midlands, and the northwest of England, and Gleneagles was a success from the word go. And for those tired of the congestion and hassle of British roads, it is still possible to travel to Gleneagles by train from most parts of the United Kingdom.

Matheson chose the perfect location for his resort, an expansive estate in glorious surroundings overlooked by the Ochil Hills and, more distantly, by the Grampian Mountains. Though it may sound mountainous, it is not so hilly as to hinder the many outdoor activities his well-heeled guests would have enjoyed: golf, shooting, fishing, riding, and walking. These have been developed and refined over the years, and today's guests at Gleneagles can fish for salmon in the River Tay and trout in the lochs of the estate, or take part in falconry or a wide variety of equestrian pursuits, from show jumping and mountain trail riding to carriage driving. The estate embraces a world-renowned shooting school, two off-road driving courses, and numerous walks and cycle trails, and after such strenuous efforts it is possible to work out even further or simply relax in the Club and Spa, with their two swimming pools, gymnasium, saunas, and Turkish bath. Having shed a few pounds, it is all too easy to gain them in one of the four restaurants (with wine lists to satisfy the most exacting of tastes). It goes without saying that guest rooms and suites are supremely comfortable in the grand Scottish country house tradition.

Currently Gleneagles has four golf courses, the par-3 Wee Course and three full-length courses, and more are planned for the future. The original courses, the King's and Queen's, opened before the hotel was finished, in 1919, and were designed by five-times Open Champion James Braid. Remaining very much as Braid built them, they offer some of the loveliest connoisseur's golf in Scotland.

THE KING'S COURSE IS SAID BY MANY TO BE JAMES BRAID'S FINEST.

At just under 6,000 yards, the Queen's Course is not long by today's standards, and par is only 68. There are four par 4s over 400 yards in length and two par 3s over 200, plus a number of borrowed greens. Its setting is simply gorgeous, and it is quite easy to see why the Queen's is loved by many every bit as much as its larger companions. Indeed, Lee Trevino once remarked of the Queen's Course: "If Heaven is as good as this, I sure hope they have some tee times left."

For over seventy years the King's Course was the pride and joy of Gleneagles. It saw many professional tournaments played over it, and television coverage made it familiar to armchair golfers the world over. Professional golf has now moved to the PGA Centenary Course, but the knowledgable golfer who appreciates classic design and golfing heritage will not want to miss the King's. Many cite this as Braid's finest creation, a cunningly designed course which uses the natural features of the land brilliantly to give any number of deceptively sited greens, and well-judged approach work is the secret to success here. That is made readily apparent on the 1st hole, with its steeply sloped, raised green. Bunkers await the timid approach, while too bold an attempt may well leave a treacherous downhill putt. The 13th, Braid's Brawest, is a celebrated long par 4, well protected by ridges and bunkers, while the 14th is a glorious reminder of the golden age of golf, when a line of cross-bunkers 140 yards from the tee once provided a

THE QUEEN'S COURSE.

serious obstacle. Now the challenge is to drive the narrow, raised green on this short par 4. It is still good fun, as is every hole on the course.

To provide a course long enough to challenge today's long-hitting professionals, Jack Nicklaus, the greatest golfer of his age, was commissioned. Called the Monarch's Course when it opened in 1993, it is now known as the PGA Centenary Course, a 7,088-yard course which has taken on the mantle of host to professional tournaments, and has already been selected to stage the 2014 Ryder Cup Matches. Sensibly, there are several sets of tees for both men and women, so those visitors who do not aspire to out-driving Tiger Woods will not find it a slog. In truth, they will be able

to savour the marvellous views from this upland site and enjoy the variety of challenges Nicklaus has set. Unusually, there are five short holes and five shortish par 5s to balance them, and the good player will hope to get up in two shots on at least four of them. There is plenty of room, too, but the design (mirroring Braid's strategic cunning on the King's and Queen's Courses) calls for thoughtful placing of every shot if a good score is to be achieved. The 1st green, for instance, is angled from left to right and protected by bunkers on either side, so the ideal place for the drive is down the left of the fairway to leave an open approach shot. At 516 yards from the tournament tees, the 2nd is not long as par 5s go, but again the drive must be precisely placed in the right-hand part of the fairway if there is to be any chance of hitting the green in two, for the green is narrow and rises to the left round a bunker and a lake. Even the less ambitious must place their second shots on the right, short of the green, to give a pitch shot down the length of the green.

Nicklaus was one of the longest hitters of his age, so it is perhaps no surprise that the 4th hole is named after him, Gowden Beastie or Golden Bear. It is the longest of the par 3s — 239 yards off the back tee — but the green curls to the left behind an expansive bunker, not really favouring the high fade which was Nicklaus's trademark shot. Following it, the 5th is one of the strongest holes on the course, with an undulating and

THE PGA CENTENARY COURSE WILL HOST THE RYDER CUP MATCHES IN 2014.

LOCH-AN EERIE STANDS BESIDE THE 13TH AND 14TH HOLES OF THE QUEEN'S COURSE.

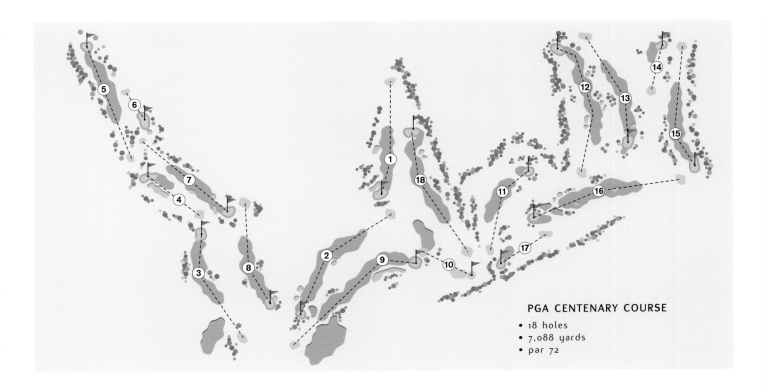

PGA CENTENARY COURSE
- 18 holes
- 7,088 yards
- par 72

tree-lined fairway. Only the confident drive down the left, skirting the trees, but that is the side to be in order to find the narrow entrance to the green.

Outright length is not always essential on the PGA Centenary Course, a case in point being the 350-yard 11th. Here again, placing of the tee shot is the key, with a burn crossing the fairway just in front of the green, and the putting surface is angled to the right, closely guarded by bunkers and far from easy to read. Then comes the shortest of the par 5s, only 503 yards from the very back. Once more the drive must be precise, for the fairway narrows and is bunkered where the ideal tee shot lands, and the second shot must

avoid a very obvious bunker on the front left of the green, which can force the unwary into straying a little to the right where there are further bunkers. Tactics on the PGA Centenary Course are no less vital than on the other two courses. This is particularly true of the 463-yard 15th, where the drive must be held right to avoid rolling off into a wicked depression on the left, and also to create the best angle to approach this narrow, heavily bunkered green. With two par 5s sandwiching a short hole, the professionals expect to pick up shots on the closing stretch, but less gifted players will find the challenge goes on to the very end, with clear thinking required on each shot.

Contact:

The Gleneagles Hotel
Auchterarder
Perthshire
Scotland PH3 1NF
Tel +44 (0)1764 662231
Email: resort.sales@gleneagles.com
www.gleneagles.com

St. Andrews, Fife, Scotland

Golf has been a way of life for the townsfolk of St. Andrews since the 15th century. A decree of 1552 granted citizens the right to raise rabbits on the links and 'play at golf, football and shuteing... with all manner of pastimes', to dig for shells, and even to dry their washing on the gorse bushes. The Old Course, the most famous golf course in the world, begins and ends in the town, and locals habitually meet by the railings to chat and cast a knowledgable eye over the steady stream of golfers coming and going. Buckets and spades, kites and bathing costumes are carried by families as they make their way along Granny Clark's Wynd, heading for the West Shore, causing golfers on the 1st and 18th to stop playing until the strollers are safely out of range. Golf is important in St. Andrews, but there is much more to the city than golf.

St. Andrews is a tiny city by today's standards, and home to Scotland's oldest university, founded in 1410. Its (now ruined) cathedral was once the metropolitan see of Scotland and a place of pilgrimage, and its narrow streets have managed to retain their mix of elegant housing and thriving shops, in an age when out-of-town superstores have sounded the deathknell for small shops in many towns and cities.

The clubhouse of the Royal and Ancient Golf Club founded in 1754, dominates the scene, overlooking the Old Course from its lofty perch above the 1st tee and final green. Contrary to popular belief, the 'R&A' does not own the six St. Andrews courses, which are in fact owned by the city and administered for it by the St. Andrews Links Trust. For the most part, golfers can simply turn up, pay a modest green fee, and play. Unfortunately, getting a round on the Old Course is not so simple. It is possible to book two years in advance! There is also a daily ballot, golfers putting their names down the day before they want to play and keeping their fingers crossed for good fortune. Single players may present themselves at the Starter's box and hope to be joined with a pair or three-ball. However, to guarantee a round it is simplest and best to book through the Old Course Experience, which has a commercial arrangement with the Links Trust, providing reservations for prime tee times. The Old Course Experience has links with several of the prominent hotels in St. Andrews, not least the Old Course Hotel, Golf Resort and Spa.

Of the many hotels in St. Andrews, none is more conspicuously connected with the Old Course than the Old Course Hotel, for drives at the 17th hole are made over part of it! The hotel now stands where once there were railway sheds, and ever since the construction of the railway in the mid-19th century the only hope a golfer has of making a par on the 17th has been to drive out over those sheds to find the elusive fairway. The contours of that part of the hotel over which the drive is made have been shaped specially to recreate the demands of hitting over the old sheds.

OPPOSITE: THE SWILCAN BRIDGE WITH THE CLUBHOUSE OF THE ROYAL AND ANCIENT GOLF CLUB ON THE LEFT, AND THE SHARED FAIRWAY OF THE 1ST AND 18TH HOLES OF THE OLD COURSE, ST. ANDREWS.

RIGHT: HELL BUNKER, 14TH HOLE, THE OLD COURSE.

In addition to giving access to the public courses of St. Andrews, The Old Course Hotel has its own course, the Duke's, a few miles away at Craigtoun Park. Designed by five-times Open Champion Peter Thomson, it gives superb views over the city and far out to sea.

In truth, this part of Fife is simply littered with great golf: Kingsbarns, the spectacular new and highly-acclaimed links designed by the American Kyle Phillips; Crail, the seventh oldest golf club in the world, with two contrasting courses, The Old designed by Old Tom Morris and Craighead, a recent creation by another American, Gil Hanse; Elie, where James Braid grew up and learned his golf; Lundin and Leven, a pair of fine links courses sharing a common boundary; Scotscraig, a demanding heathland course used for Open Championship final qualifying rounds; Ladybank, an admirable and testing inland course with incomparable turf; and Dunfermline, with its 600-year old clubhouse and links to the beginnings of golf in America, for it was former members of this club who founded the St. Andrews Club at Yonkers in New York.

What makes the Old Course so special? Many have stood on the 1st tee for the first time and wondered what all the fuss was about. One who did was the great Bobby Jones. He hated it so much he tore up his card during the 1921 Open Championship and stormed off the course. But he returned, in time learning the subtleties which give the Old Course

PUTTING ON THE 18TH GREEN OF THE OLD COURSE.

its greatness. He grew to love it so much that towards the end of his life he declared, "I could take out of my life everything except my experiences at St. Andrews and I'd still have a rich, full life."

The 1st tee looks out over what must be the widest fairway in the world, shared with the 18th, with nothing to prevent a solid drive other than the golfer's own 1st tee nerves. A strong player might almost drive the green, were it not for the Swilcan Burn which cuts across the fairway just in front of the putting surface. On the 2nd tee comes the first manifestation of the course's subtlety. There appears to be lots of room for the drive, with plenty of open space out to the left. A drive down the right-hand side of the fairway seems to be much riskier, with gorse bushes and a sprinkling of bunkers awaiting the slightest error. Yet that is the side to be if the hole is cut on the left, for the moundwork and bunkering on the approach to the green leave an

impossible shot from the left, or else a putt of enormous length, for this is the first of seven double greens. Over the next few holes it soon becomes apparent that this is a course which does not easily yield to powerful play. Thoughtful play is what is required. True, Open Championships at St. Andrews have been won by powerful players such as Jack Nicklaus, Severiano Ballesteros, John Daly, and Tiger Woods, but it was Woods's brilliant game plan and perfect execution of it which brought him the 2000 Championship in such an emphatic manner. He realized that the key to success was to avoid the bunkers — there are hundreds of them on the Old Course — and by playing supremely intelligent golf he contrived not to go into a single bunker during the course of his four rounds, enabling him to win by a comfortable 8-stroke margin.

Seen from above, the Old Course resembles a shepherd's crook, stretching away from the town with a loop at the far end.

PART OF THE RUINS OF ST. ANDREWS CATHEDRAL, WITH THE TOWER OF ST. SALVATOR'S COLLEGE BEYOND.

This loop begins with a hole, the 7th, so typical of the Old Course with multiple ways of playing it, depending largely on the strength and direction of the wind and where the hole has been cut. The green, shared with the 11th, is wonderfully sited on top of a dune overlooking the Eden Estuary, but the golfer's eyes will need to be focused on the putting surface, for this is a wickedly contoured affair and downhill putts are the stuff of white knuckles. It is no less demanding when the green is visited again at the 11th. But of greater concern are the two bunkers, Hill and Strath (every single bunker on the Old Course has a name), lurking below the green, "so deep you can get lost in them".

Bunkers — or avoiding them — will be the key to success on the run in from here. There do not appear to be any as you look from the 12th tee, but in fact the fairway is littered with them. Strong men might drive out over the top of them, but the rest of us must play safely to the side of them, leaving a tricky approach shot. Looking back from the green all the bunkers are plainly visible, a vestige of the fact that the Old Course used to be played backwards. It still is once a year, in a unique opportunity for golfing historians.

Perhaps the best-known bunker is Hell, a vast sandy cavern governing the entire strategy of the long 14th. Its very presence is often enough to cause golfers to stray into some of the other bunkers on the hole: the Beardies, Kitchen, or Grave.

PLAYERS MUST DRIVE OVER THE OLD COURSE HOTEL TO FIND THE 17TH FAIRWAY.

THE GREEN IS TO THE RIGHT OF THE SCOREBOARD IN THE DISTANCE.

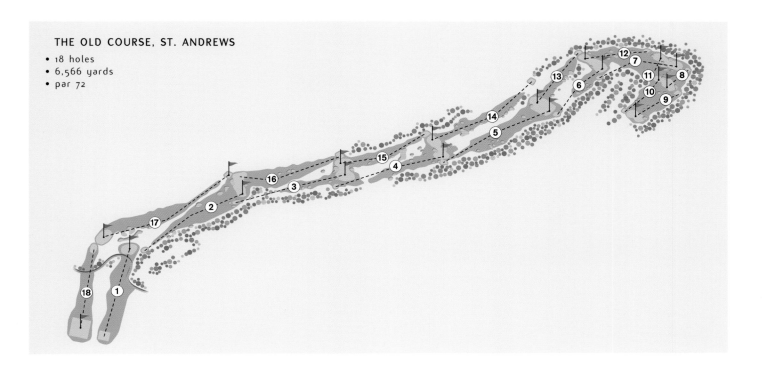

THE OLD COURSE, ST. ANDREWS
- 18 holes
- 6,566 yards
- par 72

And it is a single bunker which dictates play on the treacherous 17th, the Road Hole. The green is raised up, a long, angled table top and no easy target. On the right side it falls sharply to a metalled road (in play) and a stone wall beyond. On the left is a deep pit, the terrifying Road Bunker. From under its steep face escape may not be possible in the direction of the green, or else the deftest of touches is required to get out of the bunker without careering over the narrow green to finish hard up against the stone wall. A catalogue of great golfers have seen their championship hopes dashed on this 71st hole of the Open Championship.

First-time visitors to the Old Course are strongly advised to use the services of a caddie. Not only do they give wise counsel on the best lines to take on drives and approach shots and the reading of putts on these very deceptive surfaces, but also they have witnessed all the marvellous — and disastrous — shots played by the great players in championships, and by the celebrities who come here every autumn for the dunhill links championships. It is so heartening after playing a good shot somewhere on the course to be told, "I saw so-and-so play from that very spot in the Open. He wound up in that bunker there, took two to get out and missed the cut by one."

The Westin Turnberry Resort,
Ayrshire, Scotland

To stand on a summer's evening on the terrace below Turnberry's famous hotel as the reddest of suns sinks into the Firth of Clyde is to experience something very special. The eye is drawn out to the west over the two fine golf courses, past the lighthouse, towards the Isle of Arran and the Mull of Kintyre and, inevitably, further down the coast to that extraordinary 340-metre (1,000-ft) rocky prominence rising abruptly from the ocean like a giant sea monster, Ailsa Craig. But those who stood here in the 1940s were scanning the skies for enemy planes. Below them there were few vestiges of golf, amid a mass of concrete, tarmac, and hangars. Turnberry had become a military aerodrome, its hotel a military hospital. In the days of food rationing and national poverty following the Second World War, it took great vision and stubborn perseverance to restore Turnberry to something that even managed to exceed its former greatness.

Golf first came to Turnberry in 1901 when the Marquess of Ailsa had a little 9-hole course laid out there. The Glasgow and South-Western Railway took it over a couple of years later, extending its tracks south from Ayr and building a station and hotel in 1906. Importantly, it also engaged Willie Fernie of Troon to construct two golf courses, which opened in 1909. This was the first golf resort in Britain, and it was not the last to be developed by a railway company, Cruden Bay and Gleneagles being other notable examples. Prominence was soon brought to it by the Ladies' British Open Championship, held at Turnberry for the first time in 1912. These courses did not flourish for long, however, as the land was taken over by the Royal Flying Corps as a training ground for its pilots during the First World War. A war memorial overlooking the 9th and 12th greens of today's Ailsa Course reminds us what a dangerous business flying was in those pioneering days.

After the Great War a new golf course was built and one of the old ones restored, and another period of golfing distinction began, only to be far more seriously shattered by the wholesale destruction of the courses during the Second World War. With the coming of peace in 1945 there seemed very little prospect of being able to salvage anything of the hotel or golf courses, and it was only through the extreme doggedness and determination of one Frank Hole, Managing Director of British Transport Hotels (the new owners of Turnberry), that Philip Mackenzie Ross was engaged in 1949 to start all over again, attempting to create a golf course out of a jumble of concrete and corrugated iron.

Before the war, Ross had been a partner of the eccentric Tom Simpson and had worked with him on the design of courses throughout Europe. Simpson's instinctive understanding of the elements of good strategic design enabled him to create some of continental Europe's greatest courses, and Ross shared many of Simpson's qualities apart from his eccentricity. Interestingly, at about the time Ross was working wonders at Turnberry, he was also working a miracle of a different kind a few miles away (as the crow flies) at Southerness on the Dumfriesshire coast. Golfing visitors to southern Scotland are warmly urged to acquaint themselves with this quiet and remote links gem which shows just what a brilliant course can be built on a minuscule budget.

TURNBERRY HAS ONE OF THE FINEST STRETCHES OF SEASIDE HOLES IN BRITAIN FROM THE 4TH TO THE 11TH.

CROWDS GATHER ROUND TURNBERRY'S 18TH GREEN DURING AN OPEN CHAMPIONSHIP. THE HOTEL IS IN THE BACKGROUND.

Ross achieved something quite remarkable at Turnberry. He managed to find a way through the debris to route a course, creating one of the most exhilarating stretches of seaside golf in Britain from the 4th to the 10th. The Ailsa Course enjoys grand dunes with valley fairways hidden away among them, elevated plateau tees, and greens revealing gorgeous seascapes. One of the most spectacular championship tees in Britain, the 9th, has a 200-yard carry over the pounding waves from a tee on a rocky promontory to a hump-backed fairway far in the distance. The new course opened in 1951, to be joined by a sister course, the Arran, in 1953. Ten years later the Walker Cup matches were held on the Ailsa Course, and already its name was being thrown into the hat for a future Open Championship. It came in 1977.

The record books show that Tom Watson triumphed that year, with a record low-score of 268. What they do not show is that for the final 36 holes Watson and Jack Nicklaus were locked in head-to-head combat, giving one of the most breathtaking displays of golf ever seen in a major championship. Turnberry's Open Championship history had begun with a classic. Two further Open Championships have since been held over the Ailsa Course in 1986 and 1994.

Turnberry has not rested on its laurels since then. In golfing terms, the most significant development has been Donald Steel's masterly make-over of the Arran, which has been renamed the Kintyre Course. Where the old Arran was always something of a bridesmaid to the Ailsa,

the new Kintyre is very much an equal partner, a first-rate links course by any reckoning. The recently opened Colin Montgomerie Links Golf Academy is a state-of-the-art teaching and practice facility. There is a splendid new golf clubhouse and even a pitch-and-putt course, so that those who do not golf can say that they have played at Turnberry!

With plenty of spare land between the hotel and golf courses, Turnberry is also able to offer archery, rifle shooting, a crossbow range, falconry, quad bikes, riding on the beach, and 4 x 4 driving, all on site. It hardly needs to be said that fishing is also available. This is Scotland, after all. A spa caters for those who have overdone it on the golf course or simply found the food and drink too tempting – and with a wine list like Turnberry's it is hard to resist! From Premier cru claret from the 1980s to burgundies from the Domaine de la Romanée-Conti: the wine list is outstanding and the French-inspired food complements it perfectly. Again this is Scotland, and whisky lovers will simply purr at the huge number of drams available by the glass, some of the malts dating back to the 1930s. If it is not on Turnberry's list it probably does not exist.

Within the hotel, the atmosphere is very much that of an Edwardian country house. Everything is tasteful and comfortable, grand but not overpowering. There is also a range of lodges and cottages in the grounds, offering a similar ambience within smaller units.

THE POSTAGE STAMP AT ROYAL TROON, THE SHORTEST HOLE ON ANY OPEN CHAMPIONSHIP COURSE.

A GOLFER DRIVING FROM TURNBERRY'S 9TH TEE WITH AILSA CRAIG IN THE BACKGROUND.

AILSA COURSE
- 18 holes
- 6,976 yards
- par 72

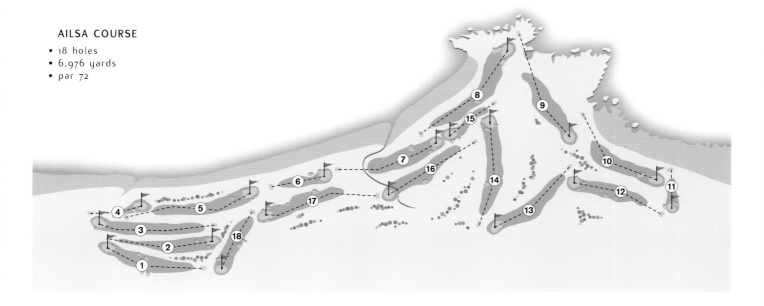

Turnberry is without a doubt the most scenic of the Open Championship venues, but it is not the only one on this fabulously well-endowed Ayrshire coast. Royal Troon has tested the world's greatest players eight times, with Arnold Palmer and Tom Watson among its victors. It is famed for the Postage Stamp, the 126-yard par-3 8th, a terrific little hole played across a valley to a diminutive green, with all manner of horrors awaiting should the ball not find the putting surface. But what makes Troon so challenging is the run home from the 10th, a series of muscular holes, very often played into the wind, where survival is more the order of the day than attack.

Prestwick hosted 24 Open Championships between 1860 and 1925, and all who care for the history and traditions of the game should make a point of visiting it, in order to acquaint themselves with its bumpy fairways, blind shots, and idiosyncratic holes, the very essence of golf in its golden age.

Were it not for Royal Troon and Turnberry, Western Gailes might well have become the Ayrshire coast's Open venue. It is a lovely course, charming yet testing. Nearby is one of the few new links courses in Scotland, Dundonald. Although it is a strictly private club, a few tee times are available for visitors. Other worthwhile links courses in the area include Irvine, Kilmarnock (Barassie), Glasgow Gailes, and the three municipal courses at Troon — Lochgreen, Darley, and Fullarton. Finally, those who look for a little romance in their golf should take the ferry to Arran and play Shiskine, one of seven very entertaining courses on the island.

Golf in and around Turnberry:

Westin Turnberry Resort
Turnberry, Ayrshire
Scotland
KA26 9LT
Tel: +44 (0)1655 331000
Email: turnberry@westin.com
www.turnberry.co.uk

Royal Troon Golf Club
Craigend Road, Troon
Ayrshire, Scotland
KA10 6EP
Tel: +44 (0)1292 311555
Email: bookings@royaltroon.com
www.royaltroon.co.uk

Prestwick Golf Club
2 Links Road, Prestwick
Ayrshire, Scotland
KA9 1QG
Tel: +44 (0)1292 671020
Email: bookings@prestwickgc.co.uk
www.prestwickgc.co.uk

Western Gailes Golf Club
Gailes, Irvine
Ayrshire, Scotland
KA11 5AE
Tel: +44 (0)1294 311649
Email: enquiries@westerngailes.com
www.westerngailes.com

Fancourt Hotel and Country Club Estate, George, South Africa

South Africa has a long and distinguished golfing history. As in many other parts of the former British Empire, British (mostly Scottish) soldiers, merchants, engineers, and doctors introduced the game, along with soccer, tennis, rugby, cricket, and other sports in which the British excelled at that time. The first South African course was a 9-hole layout near Cape Town, made by British troops in 1882. The inaugural national Amateur Championship was held at Kimberley in 1892, and since then South Africa has produced many world-class players. This was especially true in the years after the Second World War, when Bobby Locke was one of the dominant figures, winning the Open Championship four times. Following him, Gary Player became one of only five players to achieve the Grand Slam of Majors (Masters, US Open, Open Championship, and USPGA) becoming a major presence on the world golfing stage for many years. Today Ernie Els and Retief Goosen proudly carry the flag for South African golf with great success and nobility.

Early golf courses in South Africa were fairly primitive. Grass did not grow easily, and many of these courses had compacted sand greens. Today's South African courses, by contrast, are among the best-conditioned in the world. Science and technology have made it possible to grow perfect golfing turf (for fairways, greens, and tees) whether thousands of feet up in the Transvaal or at sea level in Cape Town or Durban. In addition, golf tourism is a fairly recent activity in South Africa — really only since the downfall of the loathsome apartheid system — and its golf resorts are not (yet) overwhelmed with visitors in the same way as St. Andrews or Pebble Beach. Now is the time to golf in South Africa, before the rest of the world catches on to what is on offer there.

The name Fancourt originates from Henry Fancourt White, who built a house at the foot of the Outeniqua Mountains in the 1850s. Although it has had many owners and plenty of ups and downs since then, it still stands. In 1987, Fancourt's then owner decided to convert the estate into a hotel and golf courses. They were not wholly successful, and it took another purchase of the estate — in 1994 by a German couple, the software magnates Hasso and Sabine Plattner — to set it up on the footing it has achieved today. The Manor House is now at the centre of the estate's accommodation, gently restored to preserve its mid-19th-century elegance and charm. It has only 34 bedrooms, so most guests stay in garden rooms or lodges within the grounds. The gardens are one of Fancourt's most remarkable resources. Originally they were rather dull and formal, but Sabine Plattner spearheaded a move to introduce an element of wildness. A fortune has been spent on transplanting trees and raising flowers and foliage plants from cuttings and seed, and the gardens have now become an important collection in their own right, not only providing the most beautiful surroundings for Fancourt but also acting as a reference collection of all that can be grown in this part of Africa.

THE LINKS COURSE AT FANCOURT REPLICATES MANY OF THE FEATURES OF TRADITIONAL SCOTTISH LINKS COURSES, SUCH AS POT BUNKERS AND UNDULATING FAIRWAYS.

ALL FOUR COURSES AT FANCOURT SHARE THE MAJESTIC BACKDROP OF THE OUTENIQUA MOUNTAINS.

Gracious living has always been a part of Fancourt's heritage, and its five restaurants continue that tradition, from the Italian cuisine of La Cantina in the Manor House itself to Morning Glory which serves light, healthy meals overlooking the Outeniqua Course. Seafood is the speciality of Le Pêcheur in the main clubhouse, while Bramble Lodge, next to the Links Course, serves "global fusion cuisine". Finally, back in the Manor House is Sansibar, where the cuisine represents the best of modern African styles. Indoor and outdoor swimming, bowls, croquet, tennis, and volleyball are among the sports on offer, and horseback riding is available from the equestrian centre. The gardens and local walks are well worth exploring, for Fancourt is very much at one with nature, and the birdlife, in particular, is magnificent.

To help visitors to get away from it all, Fancourt also offers a private lodge, Glentana, high on the cliffs overlooking the Indian Ocean. Though only half an hour's drive away, it guarantees honeymooners or important decision-makers total seclusion and high comfort in a dramatic setting. The resort's conference facilities are extensive, and include a banqueting hall with the capacity to seat 350 guests.

Four golf courses make up the roster at Fancourt, three of them exclusively for the use of Fancourt members and resort guests. The public-play facility, Bramble Hill, is the newest of the courses. With its kikuyu grass fairways and bent grass greens and tees, there is something of a links feel to this 6,300 yard course, designed by the Gary Player team to provide "golfers of every level a Fancourt experience". Soon after it opened the Montagu Course got on the radar of South African golf, climbing to the number one spot in the country in the year 2000. It has recently been upgraded by David McClay Kidd, currently one of the most fashionable designers in world golf course construction, noted for his exquisite course at Bandon Dunes in Oregon. The Montagu provides a stiff test from the back plates, when the course measures over 7,200 yards, with plentiful water hazards. Both the Montagu and Outeniqua Courses have been lauded for their exceptionally high maintenance standards over their (admittedly brief) lives. Outeniqua is also a Gary Player design, stretching to around 7,000 yards with plenty of challenge.

The Links at Fancourt is the jewel in a remarkably lustrous crown. It, too, is a Gary Player design, and he and his team

GARDEN SUITES AND STUDIOS COMPLEMENT THE MORE TRADITIONAL ACCOMMODATION TO BE FOUND IN THE MANOR HOUSE.

were given an inauspicious piece of ground on which to work. "I feel this is one of the very best golf courses in the world," observed Player (never one to undersell himself!), "even though it may have been built on the worst piece of ground." Hasso Plattner asked Player for a course with links-like characteristics, to contrast with the more park-like Montagu and Outeniqua. "It has been designed to

make golfers feel as though they were at Ballybunion, Dornoch or St. Andrews, with rolling fairways, pot bunkers, big greens, high rough and a seascape appearance," wrote Player. Thousands and thousands of tons of clay were manoeuvred by heavy-duty earth-movers and bulldozers in order to create the natural-looking dunes which border, and sometimes interrupt, the fairways. Such is the vigour of the

mounds and humps that have been created that they tie in superbly with the rugged mountain scenery surrounding this course.

Although it opened only in 2000, the Links at Fancourt has seen much top-level tournament golf, including the 2003 President's Cup, an event played every two years between teams of professionals

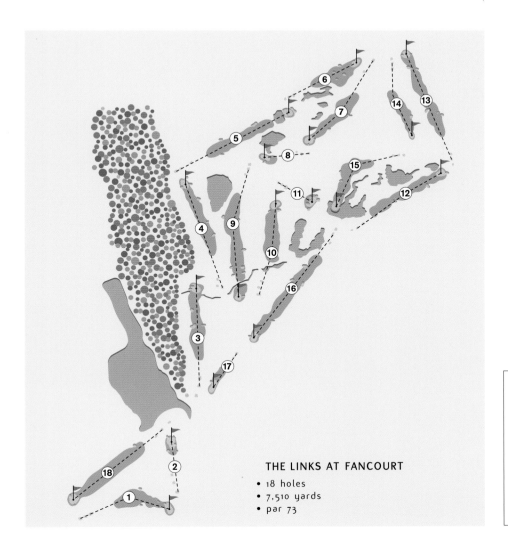

THE LINKS AT FANCOURT
- 18 holes
- 7,510 yards
- par 73

Contact:

Fancourt Hotel and Country Club Estate
PO Box 2266
George
6530
South Africa
Tel: +27 (0)44 804 0000
Email: hotel@fancourt.co.za
www.fancourt.co.za

from the United States and the rest of the world (except Europe, which has the Ryder Cup). Those old adversaries Jack Nicklaus and Gary Player were the respective team captains, and many of the world's finest players were involved, including Tiger Woods, Phil Mickelson, Ernie Els, and Retief Goosen. On the last day it all came down to the final match, with Australia's Robert Allenby beating

America's Davis Love III on the final hole to halve the match. Then it was a sudden death play-off, with Els and Woods head-to-head in match-play. After three holes they had not been separated, and with darkness falling the two team captains agreed to halve the contest, in one of the most exciting match-play events ever witnessed. It will surely not be the last big event played on this majestic links.

San Roque Club, Cádiz, Spain

With players of the calibre of Severiano Ballesteros, José Maria Olazábal, Miguel Angel Jiménez and Sergio Garcia, Spain has been a major force in professional golf for the past quarter-century or so. At the same time dozens of new courses have sprung up all along the Spanish coast, from Catalonia in the northeast to Cádiz in the southwest. Before that there was very little golf in Spain, and certainly no holiday golf. Spain's first golf course was established not on the mainland but on the Canary Islands in 1891. The first mainland club was Puerta de Hierro, a private club on the hills behind the university of Madrid, overlooking the city centre. It has a fine principal course, but is strictly members only. Other clubs were few and far between, and mainly in the north: San Sebastian (1910), Neguri (1911), Zarauz (1916), and Sant Cugat (1914). Real Pedreña, where Ballesteros first played, was one of the few clubs set up in the inter-war years, in 1922. Golf in Spain was the preserve of a few wealthy enthusiasts and overseas diplomats and businessmen. In the south, the Club de Campo at Málaga (1925) remained something of a lonely outpost.

No survey of golf in Spain would be complete without mention of Javier Arana, Spain's first native golf course architect, who began designing courses about the time of the Spanish Civil War (1936–9). Between then and the 1960s he created a number of jewels, notably the Club de Campo in Madrid, the original El Prat in Barcelona, and El Saler outside Valencia, his masterpiece which was consistently rated as one of the top ten courses in continental Europe for many years. In 1959 he made the trip south to construct a course in Andalucía, the original 18 holes at Guadalmina. But it went largely unnoticed, partly because tourism had barely touched this far south, and partly because Arana was unknown outside Spain. He never worked in any another country and it is only in more recent years that his courses have gained international recognition for their merits.

It was left to the giant of the post-war years, Robert Trent Jones, to establish big-time golf in the south, which he did with Sotogrande (1964) and Las Brisas (1968). These two led a march which has turned into a stampede, with new courses opening at an extraordinary rate. Both Sotogrande and Las Brisas are private courses, although they do accept a limited number of visiting golfers — at a price! Trent Jones's other famous course in this region, Valderrama, has stolen the limelight in recent years by hosting the 1997 Ryder Cup, and by bringing together the stars of the US and European tours for the American Express Championships.

Northern Europeans have been flocking to southern Spain since the 1970s, notably to escape their dark and cold winters, and many have chosen to make their homes there. While some of the new hotels and private dwellings imitate the style of traditional Andalucían buildings, there is a great deal of very average construction and the coastal strip either side of the notorious N340 trunk road is now a ribbon development of ever-expanding width. Get into the hinterland, however, and the towns and villages of Andalucía and the province of Cádiz retain their characteristic charm, the countryside is delightful, and the restaurants and bars still cater to Spanish tastes, not those of fast food and junk food. The beautiful pueblos blancos (white towns or villages, so-named after their whitewashed Moorish architecture) are a particular delight.

TREES AT SAN ROQUE PROVIDE WELCOME RELIEF FROM THE INTENSE HEAT OF SOUTHERN SPAIN.

THE VOLVO MASTERS, A PRINCIPAL EVENT ON THE EUROPEAN TOUR, HAS BEEN PLAYED IN SOUTHERN SPAIN — AT MONTECASTILLO OR VALDERRAMA SINCE 1988.

The city of Cádiz is also not be missed. One of Europe's oldest cities and great trading ports, Cádiz is the centre of sherry wine export, and those with a liking for sherry should not miss a visit to one (or more) of the sherry bodegas in Jerez de la Frontera. Manzanilla is made overlooking the coast at Sanlucar de Barrameda, the sea apparently giving this particular sherry its slightly salty tang. And no visit to this part of Spain would be complete without seeing Seville,

Spain's third largest city and one of its most handsome. The enormous 15th-century cathedral (the largest Gothic cathedral in the world), the Plaza de Aspaña (designed as the centrepiece of the Spanish Americas Fair), the neo-Moorish Alcázar and the old Jewish Quarter of Santa Cruz are absolute musts. Granada, too, is worthy of a whole day's trip. Its great palace, the Alhambra, is breathtaking both in its magnificence — with stunning gardens, pools, fountains, and cascades — and its hill-top setting,

offering commanding views for miles around. Take time to walk up the hill next to the Alhambra into the Albaicin, the old Moorish casbah with its labyrinth of tiny streets, and inexpensive restaurants serving the best of local dishes.

Situated close to Gibraltar and between Sotogrande and Valderrama is the San Roque Club. At the heart of the club is the old mansion of the Domecq family, the famous sherry dynasty.

MOST OF SAN ROQUE IS PLAYED ON THE FLAT, BUT THAT DOES NOT MEAN THAT IT IS ANY EASIER.

This ravishingly beautiful house is perfectly Andalucían in style, with courtyards and Moorish arcades providing cool shade from the searing midday sun. The 50 guest rooms and 50 hacienda-style suites are exquisitely furnished and built in the local materials of stone, terracotta, oak and cork.

Spanish cooking tends to be simpler than its French equivalent, relying more on really good ingredients and letting them speak for themselves. At San Roque, Spanish cuisine is elevated to a higher plane, with game, top-quality meats and seafood very much to the fore in the Bolero and Buganvilla restaurants, both of which feature outdoor terraces for moonlit dining. The Kamakura, reputed to be the finest Japanese restaurant in Spain, provides a complete contrast, while the tapas available at the bar are frequently served to the accompaniment of flamenco music and dancing.

As renowned as San Roque's golf courses is its equestrian centre, which preserves the traditions of Andalucían horsemanship. The Asprey Summer Event features show-jumping at the highest level. Since 2003 two golf courses have been available to San Roque guests: the Old Course, laid out by the British designer Dave Thomas, and the New Course, designed by Perry Dye

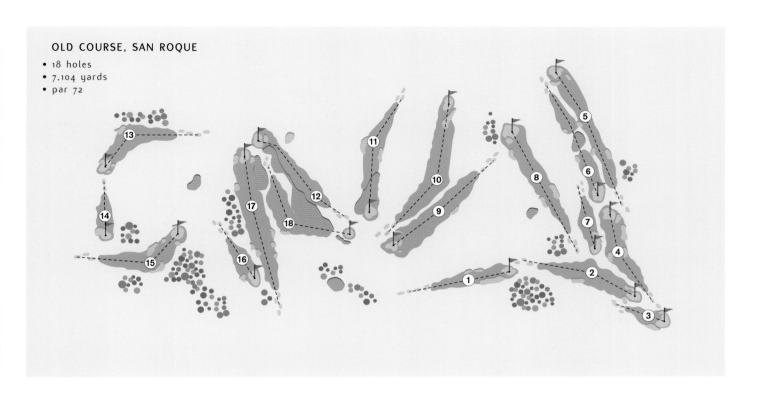

OLD COURSE, SAN ROQUE

- 18 holes
- 7,104 yards
- par 72

with input from Severiano Ballesteros. At 7,249 yards from the back tee markers, the New Course is a serious test; it has been built to accommodate golfers of all abilities, however, so there are multiple tees and the fairways are generally wider than on the Old Course. Roaming gently hilly ground above the resort, it offers wide panoramas and glimpses of the Mediterranean.

The Old Course, a frequent venue for the European Tour Qualifying School, is set on flatter ground, apart from a stretch on the back nine which navigates round a hill. Dave Thomas consulted past-Open Champion Tony Jacklin on the design, which makes great demands

on driving and, in particular, approach work, and from the back tees, when it plays to 7,104 yards, it is technically very challenging. Water is used sparingly, with only the 6th troubled by it on the front nine. However, the 11th and 12th are entirely dependent upon the strategic use of water and it returns to dominate the 17th and 18th. The greens are generously sized and the bunkering is expansive. It is not easy to keep golf courses in first-class condition in the hot, dry environment of Andalucía, but the expertise and hard work of the dedicated team at San Roque ensures that both courses are always in peak condition.

Contact:

The San Roque Club
C.N. 340 KM 127
11360 San Roque (Cádiz)
Spain
Tel: +34 956 613 030
Email: info@sanroqueclub.com
www.sanroqueclub.com

The American Club,
Kohler, Wisconsin, USA

It is somewhat incongruous that one of America's most luxurious resorts should have its origins in an iron and steel foundry. John Michael Kohler was an Austrian immigrant who purchased the Sheboygan Union Iron and Steel foundry in 1873. At first the company was involved in making metal parts for agriculture and furniture. Soon it branched out into household plumbing, and the family company remains a leader in the industry to this day. Sheboygan lies on the western shores of Lake Michigan, roughly halfway between Green Bay and Milwaukee, and the Kohler family, following the example of other European industrialists, was at pains to ensure a good quality of life for its employees. In the early years of the 20th century, Walter Kohler established Kohler Village, influenced by European model villages, as a place 'where simple things, done well, will never be out of style'. Today the village forms the hub of the Kohler resort, where good living and environmental concerns rub shoulders harmoniously.

THE 2004 US PGA CHAMPIONSHIP WAS FOUGHT OUT OVER THE STRAITS COURSE AT WHISTLING STRAITS.

Kohler is not just a golf resort — far from it. In addition to its four fine golf courses, two of them internationally famous, from spring to fall it also offers riding, canoeing, fishing, and shooting among outdoor sports, plus birdwatching and country walking for nature lovers. Winter in Wisconsin is bitterly cold, and in these months cross-country skiing, dog sledding, ice skating, ice fishing, and snowshoeing are the order of the day. Museums and galleries and a wide variety of speciality shops, plus a year-long programme of events such as food and wine festivals, ensure that every non-golfing moment is easily and pleasurably filled. Moreover, the Kohler Waters Spa is on site to restore body and mind after a long day's golf.

No fewer than 28,696 yards of golf are available on the four courses at Kohler, all designed by the renowned architect Pete Dye. His courses have hosted many prestigious events in recent years including the Heritage held annually at Harbour Town, the 1988 PGA (Oak Tree), 1991 Ryder Cup (Kiawah Island), and the PGA Tour's own Players Championship which takes place each year at Sawgrass in Florida over Dye's innovative Stadium Course. These courses alone could hardly be more different and Dye could never be said to design by numbers. His inspiration always comes from the individual piece of land on which he is working, and the four courses here are very different from each other, providing a wonderfully varied golfing experience all within close proximity.

The two courses at Blackwolf Run were the first to open, back in 1988. Here the River Course was laid out in a glaciated valley, and Dye took full advantage of the rivers and lakes occupying the land, with water hazards occurring on 14 of the 18 holes. The Meadow Valleys Course played host to the 1998 US Women's Open Championship, which was won by Se Ri Pak of Korea in a score of 290, the highest winning score in more than a decade, and proof, if it were needed, of the considerable challenge of this layout. On this course, the front nine occupies rolling, open country, while the back nine descends to one of the river valleys shared with the River Course. Meadow Valleys is consistently highly ranked among public access courses in the USA by the golfing press.

NEITHER COURSE AT BLACKWOLF RUN IS OVERSHADOWED BY ITS STABLEMATES AT WHISTLING STRAITS. BOTH THE RIVER AND MEADOW VALLEYS COURSES ARE CHALLENGING IN A CHARMING ENVIRONMENT.

Ten years later, the two courses at Whistling Straits were first unveiled to the world, 14 km (9 miles) northeast of the village of Kohler on the shores of Lake Michigan. Here Dye created an Irish Course and what might be termed a Scottish course, known as the Straits Course. The Irish Course is slightly inland, and wanders through meadowland to which Dye has given "Irish-style" character

with the use of towering dunes and deep, serious bunkers. Lakes and streams abound, and there is considerable variety in the styles and challenges of the individual holes throughout the round.

But it is the Straits Course that has received the highest plaudits, as host to the 2004 USPGA Championship and 2007 US Senior Open. The 2004 USPGA turned

out to be a dramatic affair, as nerves and the course took their toll on many of the big names who had been in contention at the start of the last day. In the end, Fijian Vijay Singh and Americans Chris di Marco and Justin Leonard finished tied for the lead, necessitating a play-off which Singh won comfortably, but the course had bitten back following some low scoring in the early rounds. Singh's last round of

76, four over par, was the worst winning score for 66 years! The Straits Course played tough that day!

The Straits Course sets off with a mid-length par 4 of 405 yards through undulating dunes. The Scottish scene is set. Huge sand dunes overlook the right of the par-5 2nd hole, but the real threat for the good player is a pot-bunker 35 yards

short of the green. The 183-yard par-3 3rd introduces Lake Michigan to the strategy. Miss to the left of the green and you are in serious, aqueous trouble. It is much the same on the par-4 4th, on which both the tee shot and the approach will bounce down toward the lake. While the 5th may bring inland shelter it also offers a lake down the right side of the fairway in the landing zone and another hazard

THE 398-YARD 10TH HOLE ON THE IRISH COURSE AT WHISTLING STRAITS.

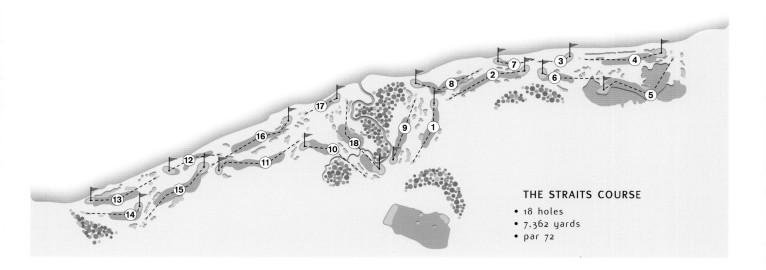

THE STRAITS COURSE
- 18 holes
- 7,362 yards
- par 72

threatens the second shot, be it a long-iron speculator or a wedge-shot banker.

On the 6th green we are back on high ground overlooking the shores of Lake Michigan, and the location of the 7th green reinforces the watery perils of missing the target here. Again, on the 8th the main preoccupation is staying dry, especially on the second shot which is played to a green perched above the lake. Returning to the clubhouse, the 9th is played down a valley between the dunes.

The 10th is very reminiscent of Scottish links golf, with its tumbling fairway, and the 11th is a monster par 5 playing to 619 yards from the very back tee, while the par-3 12th is picture postcard stuff, the green sitting on the side of a dune overlooking the lake. It is probably the trickiest of the short holes, with a deceptive putting surface that is difficult to read. Cliff Hanger is the self-explanatory

name of the par-4 13th, which takes play to the farthest point from the clubhouse. The 14th turns for home with a sharp dog-leg, and it is said that the run in from the 15th is one of the toughest finishes in all golf, needing a long drive to set up any sort of feasible approach to a heavily bunkered green. Of the par 5s the 16th is the shortest, well in range of two shots for all the pros, but the approach is uphill over rough ground to an exposed green overlooking Lake Michigan. It is followed by a devilish short hole with a big drop to bunkers on the left and dunes and bunkers guarding the high right side. This is not a green to miss! At 489 yards, the final hole is a long par 4 with length from the tee limited by a creek that crosses the fairway. The green is enormous, very undulating, and presents any number of testing pin positions. Any golfer matching his or her handicap over this testing course will have played exceptionally well.

Contact:

The American Club
444 Highland Drive
Kohler
Wisconsin 53044
USA
Tel: +1 (800) 344 2838 Ext 700
Email via: www.destinationkohler.com

The Greenbrier, West Virginia, USA

When the Ryder Cup Matches were held at the Greenbrier in 1979, the resort was already 201 years old. Ever since 1778, people had been coming to White Sulphur Springs to "take the waters" for their health. The spring is still there, under the dome of the white-columned Springhouse, the symbol of this vast resort. In the 18th century few ventured this far off the beaten track, deep in the forests of the Allegheny Mountains. Eventually a stagecoach route was created, and by the 1830s wealthy judges, lawyers, merchants, and planters from the southern states had begun to spend their summers here, building rows of attractive cottages, many of which have survived to the present day. By the 1850s, White Sulphur Springs had become the most fashionable social resort in the south, and in 1858 the opening of the Grand Central Hotel provided plentiful and comfortable accommodation for visitors.

THE GREENBRIER COURSE WAS REBUILT BY JACK NICKLAUS TO HOST THE 1979 RYDER CUP.

The Civil War brought a brief hiatus to activities, but the coming of the Chesapeake and Ohio Railway, shortly after the resort reopened, brought new visitors from the north – from New York, Washington, Chicago, and Cleveland. And it was the Railway that made the next significant move, buying the resort in 1910, and adding the Greenbrier Hotel and a golf course in 1913. This was not any golf course, but one designed by Charles Blair MacDonald, the pre-eminent golf architect of the age. The following year President Woodrow Wilson and his wife spent Easter at the Greenbrier, and the resort was confirmed as one of the most fashionable in the land. Despite two World Wars and the Great Depression, the Greenbrier survived these difficult times to emerge buoyant in 1946, when the Chesapeake and Ohio Railway reacquired the resort after military occupation. They brought in one of the great interior designers of the time, Dorothy Draper, to redecorate the hotel throughout. Her distinctive style became so much a feature of the resort that it has been retained in essence ever since. Another important appointment at this time was that of Sam Snead as golf professional, a man who would carry the Greenbrier's name with pride and dignity throughout the course of a distinguished and extraordinarily lengthy career.

The Old White Hotel (as regular visitors always referred to the Grand Central) was demolished in 1922, but its ambience and some of the motifs from it live on in today's Greenbrier, which is thoroughly modern in the pampering of its guests yet mindful of its long heritage and traditions. There is now accommodation for 803 guests at the Greenbrier, from individual rooms to the four elegant estate houses which are effectively private estates within the estate. Two of these, the Valley View and President's Estate Houses, are so spacious that 200 people can be entertained in them at any one time. Top Notch Estate House was built in 1912 as the summer residence of the president of the Chesapeake and Ohio Railway, and during the Second World War it was occupied by a number of illustrious American generals, including Dwight D. Eisenhower. Foreign dignitaries, presidents, and aristocrats have favoured the Colonnade Estate House, built in the early 1800s and furnished with 18th and 19th century pieces. The resort has almost 100 guesthouses, many of them cottages built in the early 19th century and exquisitely decorated and furnished. The decorative distinction that is so much a part of Dorothy Draper's legacy runs through every room in all parts of the Greenbrier.

PLAY DURING THE 1994 SOLHEIM CUP WHICH THE AMERICANS WON HANDSOMELY, 13–7.

Dorothy Draper is also commemorated in Draper's Café, just the place to indulge in cakes, pastries, and banana splits. Sam Snead, too, is commemorated gastronomically, his name being given to the informal dining room at the golf club. At the other end of the scale, the Main Dining Room is elegant and distinguished, complementing the classic cuisine at the heart of the menu. For those who aspire to becoming more adept with the skillet, the Culinary Arts Center runs a full programme of cookery and wine courses.

With 2,600 verdant hectares (6,500 acres) of mountains and hills surrounding the resort, outdoor leisure pursuits at the Greenbrier are many and varied. Fly fishing is ever popular, and whitewater rafting pits human skills against the power of water. Falconry, shooting, and riding are reminders of traditional country sports. The physically fit can enjoy the vigorous exploration of challenging trails on mountain bikes, while the Off-Road Driving School offers a 21st-century technological solution to crossing difficult terrain. Golf has been a feature of the Greenbrier since 1913.

The oldest of the three courses at the resort is known today as the Old White Course, after the Old White Hotel, which is now defunct. Charles Blair MacDonald, who designed it, had made a detailed study of the famous old Scottish courses at the end of the 19th-century. His masterpiece, the National Golf Links of America, might be considered a national monument, with holes that are clearly influenced by what he had observed in Scotland. While the terrain at the Greenbrier does not resemble a traditional links, MacDonald was able to bring to this design not so much recreations of famous holes, but rather re-interpretations of them. So the challenge of Old White's 8th is similar to that faced by golfers on the famous Redan hole at North Berwick. The 13th calls to mind the Alps at Prestwick, and the 15th is said to have been influenced by the famous 11th (Eden) on the Old Course at St. Andrews.

A STREAM WITH ATTENDANT STONE WALL GUARDS THE FRONT OF THE GREENBRIER'S 10TH HOLE.

But it would be very wrong to think that MacDonald was simply trying to build replicas. Each hole here is MacDonald's own response to the ground on which he was working, with a view to getting the most out of the natural features of the land. Typical is the closing hole, a shortish par 3, not at all common on great courses, yet MacDonald saw this as the best way to use the land on the return to the clubhouse. Romantically, this hole gave Sam Snead his very last hole-in-one, in 1995.

The Meadows Course started life as a short 9-hole course around 1910. In 1962 it was expanded to a full-length 18-hole circuit by Dick Wilson. It occupied land known as the "meadows" running beside a meandering stream. Then in 1998 Bob Cupp, who had studied under Wilson, was brought in to remodel the course. He did a very sensitive job, mostly upgrading greens, bunkers, and tees, but he also built completely new 11th and 12th holes and refashioned the old 15th as the new 17th, cleverly matching the style of the new holes to those of the Wilson classic. It is now, in the opinion of many, the hardest of the three courses at the Greenbrier. The 18th green is a double green, reminiscent of the Old Course at St. Andrews and shared with the final hole of the Greenbrier Course.

Seth Raynor designed the Greenbrier Course in 1924. In 1977, Jack Nicklaus redesigned it specially for the 1979 Ryder Cup Matches. Nicklaus captained

THE TRANQUIL SETTING OF THE GREENBRIER IS CAPTURED IN THIS VIEW OF THE 12TH HOLE.

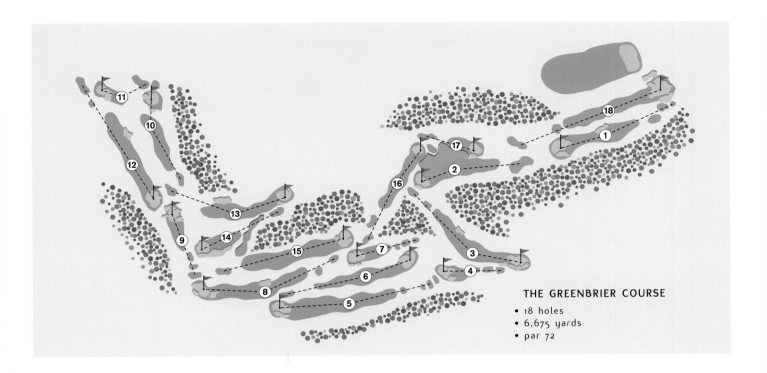

THE GREENBRIER COURSE

- 18 holes
- 6,675 yards
- par 72

the United States team, which won emphatically, 17-11. The course is blessed with great natural terrain, with undulating fairways wandering through thick forests. Water is encountered on several holes and there are a number of forced carries. Typical of the challenges set is the par-4 2nd, on which the drive must steer a safe passage between trees on one side and a lake on the other. Water again threatens on the approach to the green, and a bunker through the back of the green awaits those who err on the long side. There is no playing safe here. Another stiff test is the par-3 4th, a mid-iron shot across a valley to a plateau green protected in front by two menacing bunkers and behind by a steep downslope. Distance control is all important.

Outright length is not an issue, as the course measures only 6,675 yards from the back, but the greens are very well protected and many putting surfaces are highly contoured, and it can be set up to provide a very tricky test. In hosting the 1994 Solheim Cup, the Greenbrier became the only course to have hosted both the transatlantic professional cup tournaments, the Ryder Cup and the Solheim Cup.

Contact:

The Greenbrier
300 W. Main Street
White Sulphur Springs
West Virginia 24988
Tel: +1 (800) 453 4858
Email via www.greenbrier.com

Manele Bay Hotel & The Lodge at Koele, Hawaii, USA

Lana'i is often said to be Hawaii's most exclusive island. It prides itself on what it does not offer, notably crowds and traffic. Most of its tiny population live in Lana'i City (rather less a city than a small town or large village), built as a model town in the 1920s when an American millionaire bought the island to grow pineapples. They are still grown, but much of the island remains natural and unspoiled, a forest paradise a few miles across with breathtaking scenery, one or two old fishing villages, prehistoric mysteries, and two superb sister golfing resorts, one overlooking the Pacific Ocean, the other in the heart of the hills and forest.

Sailing, deep-sea fishing, snorkelling, and scuba diving are among the water activities on offer. Anyone with an interest in tropical reef fish should visit Hulopo'e Beach, one of America's most beautiful beaches and an important marine conservation area, brimming with brightly coloured fish of every imaginable shape and hue. Spinner dolphins and humpback whales are often to be seen further off shore, while those who venture inland into the guava forests and ironwood groves, either in a 4x4 vehicle or on a mountain bike, will be treated to glimpses of native birdlife, again in amazing variety. The forests are full of deer, too, and hunting for meat is permitted all year round. Trail rides from Koele provide an unrivalled way to explore the island's scenery, and are graded according to the experience of the rider, from absolute beginner to expert. Tennis, bowls, croquet, archery, shooting, helicopter rides, and swimming are also on the menu, but at both Manele Bay and Koele there is every excuse to do absolutely nothing except sit and drink in the beauty of the surrounding scenery.

The luxurious Lodge at Koele lies at the end of a quiet country road. There is a rustic charm to its log cabin style which blends perfectly with the forests of pines and banyans surrounding it, and there is a lovely view out over the lake to the pine-clad hills beyond. But there is nothing rustic about the facilities, which are designed to make the visitor feel especially cosseted in the true spirit of Hawaiian hospitality. Its Formal Dining Room has won awards for its contemporary New American cuisine, and the chefs both here and in the Terrace Restaurant make imaginative use of the excellent local fish, meats, vegetables, and fruits, all as fresh as can be. Even the simplest rooms are exceedingly comfortable, the suites are sumptuous, and all enjoy ravishing views.

In June 2003, Koele was named No. 1 Golf Resort in the World by *Condé Nast Traveller*, and, as might be imagined, its golf course, the Experience at Koele, is something very special. Designed by Greg Norman and Ted Robinson, it was opened in 1990, to immediate critical acclaim and awards.

THE PICTURE-POSTCARD 12TH HOLE OF THE CHALLENGE AT MANELE LOOKS SIMPLE ENOUGH FROM BEHIND THE GREEN.

A COMPLIMENTARY SHUTTLE SERVICE BRINGS RESORT GUESTS TO MANELE'S CLUBHOUSE.

From the back tees it is a serious challenge, calling for the bold ball-striking and creative skills of Norman at his peak. Less gifted golfers, playing from tees further forward, are granted an easier passage, the playability of the course being a major factor in visitors returning year after year. The course enjoys a diversity of terrains, from old pineapple fields to the deepest ravine on Lana'i, with Kiawe and Koa trees, towering pines, and eucalyptus groves, and there are glorious views across the Pacific to Maui and Molokai. From the golfing point of view, the delights of the course include its constantly changing pace, the variety of its challenges, and the routing which cleverly allows the course to build up to a remarkable finish: the amazing 17th, with a drive from a spectacular tee 76 m (250 feet) above the valley floor, and an impish short par 3 over water to end. Water plays quite a part in the design of the course, in the form of waterfalls and elaborately shaped ponds and lakes. Norman and Robinson ensured that the water features are as visually attractive as the gorgeous surroundings. Nowhere is water used more effectively than the 8th, only a short par 4, just over 300 yards, with a nerve-jangling approach shot to a green entirely surrounded by water. Shortly after it opened, Norman solved its problems dramatically by driving the green!

In 2003 *Condé Nast Traveller* found Manele Bay to be right up there with The Lodge at Koele, second in the USA and fourth in the world: a remarkable achievement for sister resorts. Perched on the cliffs overlooking Hulopo'e Beach, it offers similarly luxurious pampering for its guests. Here the cuisine has a different slant, although it too uses the finest local ingredients. The award-winning Ihilani Restaurant places the emphasis on French and Italian dishes, reflecting the Mediterranean décor and atmosphere of this serious restaurant. Hawaiian specialities, meanwhile, are the order of the day at Hulopo'e Court, Manele's striking ocean-view restaurant. There is also less formal

MANELE'S 12TH LOOKS SOMEWHAT MORE INTIMIDATING FROM THE TEE.

THE DRIVE FROM THE 17TH TEE AT KOELE PLUNGES 250 FEET TO THE VALLEY FLOOR.

eating at the poolside, in the open-air lounge and at the golf course.

Jack Nicklaus was entrusted with the design of Manele's golf course, The Challenge. The challenge for Nicklaus was to build a course that took advantage of the stunning ocean views to be had from the clifftops and hilly ground, ensuring that the ocean is never really out of view during play. An admirable objective, this could nevertheless have proved a very restrictive straightjacket. What is so noteworthy about the course is that this was achieved without compromising the best strategic use of the natural features of the site, without involving unwelcome

sidehill lies, and without requiring the golfer to make ridiculous climbs from one green to the next tee.

The Challenge gets play underway pleasantly with a fairly straightforward opening hole, the view from the green announcing immediately that this is a very special place. Sterner stuff comes on the 2nd, played uphill, round a dog-leg and over two gullies to a raised two-level green. Then comes a short hole with a compulsory carry over mesquite trees to a large green threatened by a central bunker. A careless tee shot can lead to the golfer having to putt round the bunker, dropping a silly shot at the same time.

From here the course traverses rolling ground often punctuated by gullies, and the player has to think a good deal for there are various strategic options on many shots. The long par-4 5th offers splendid views across the ocean to Maui and Kahoolawe, and to the Big Island of Hawaii. Unusually, the 7th and 8th are consecutive short holes, a feature shared with Cypress Point and Ballybunion. Generally, golf course designers try to avoid back-to-back par 3s, for a number of reasons including their potential to slow play down, but there are occasions when the opportunity to use the natural advantages of a certain part of the site is just too good to waste. The visionary architect recognizes this.

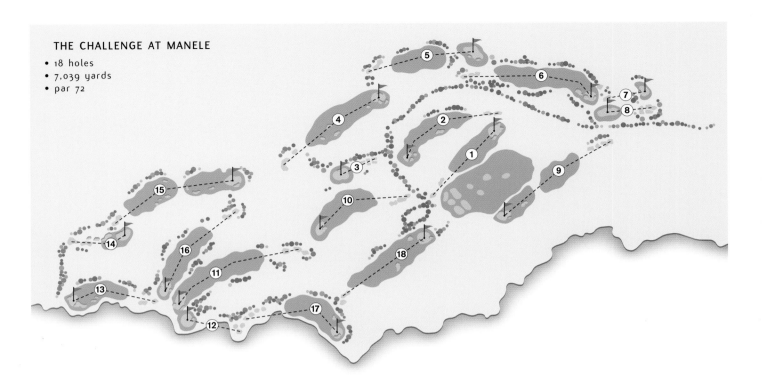

THE CHALLENGE AT MANELE

- 18 holes
- 7,039 yards
- par 72

Holes 12 and 13 are the two magnificent ocean-side holes for which Manele is particularly famed. The 11th is a sturdy par 5, the longest hole on the course at almost 590 yards. It is downhill, and requires accurate positioning of the drive and second shot, as the further the second shot is hit the more trouble it can get into. Then comes the dramatic 12th, 202 yards from the back tee, all carry over the ocean 45 m (150 ft) below. From whatever tee the hole is played it asks serious questions about club selection and needs a reliable swing. Siren-like, it is both attractive and dangerous.

After the 13th hole, the course swings inland for a few holes until regaining the

clifftops at the 16th green. The 17th, a long par 4, is the last of the ocean-side holes and a stiff test, too. There is a long carry over a rocky ravine to a narrow fairway with very little margin for error. It is all downhill from here, with accuracy again at a premium as the green is far below, set on the edge of the cliffs, with a protecting mound and bunker.

Between them the Manele Bay Hotel and The Lodge at Koele are sister resorts of the highest standards and have so much to offer of a complementary kind: their settings, their ambience, their cuisine, and their golf. What they have in common is that they are about as good as it gets in all departments.

Contact:

Manele Bay Hotel
Lana'i Resort Reservations
PO Box 630310
Lana'i City
Hawai'i 96763
Tel: +1 (808) 450 3704
Email: reservations@lanai-resorts.com
www.manelebayhotel.com

Lodge at Koele
Lana'i Resort Reservations
PO Box 630310
Lana'i City
Hawai'i 96763
Tel: +1 (808) 450 3704
Email: reservations@lanai-resorts.com
www.lodgeatkoele.com

Pebble Beach, California, USA

It is a matter of literary debate whether the inspiration for Robert Louis Stevenson's *Treasure Island* came from May Island off the east coast of Scotland or the Monterey Peninsula in California. Suffice it to say that Stevenson lived for some time near to what is now the Pebble Beach Lodge, and it seems inconceivable that the glorious scenery of this part of America's Pacific coastline should not have insinuated itself in some way into the classic story.

Pebble Beach's own story begins in 1880, when four railway tycoons opened the luxurious Del Monte Hotel near Monterey. The following year they completed the construction of 17-Mile Drive, thereby opening up this maritime wonderland to a public with a thirst for new places. Golf joined the list of pleasures available when the 9-hole Del Monte Golf Course opened for play in 1897. The oldest course west of the Mississippi, still in continuous operation on its original site, became an 18-hole course in 1903. The next significant event was the opening in 1909 of the original Lodge, at first nothing more than a log cabin. This burned down in 1917, but by then its owners, the Pacific Investment Company, had hired a young man, Samuel F.B. Morse, to develop their property holdings in the area. Morse recognized the potential of this lodge, and more particularly of the land adjoining it. The Lodge was rebuilt in stone as a comfortable place to stay, and the

Pebble Beach Golf Links was laid out on its land by Jack Neville, Douglas Grant and H. Chandler Egan. Both opened in 1919.

Although the Del Monte Hotel was badly damaged by fire in 1924, it was quickly rebuilt and proved a major factor in attracting wealthy visiting golfers from all over the United States. This was then a remote part of California, a weekend and summer retreat for the super-rich of San Francisco and Los Angeles. Nevertheless, the United States Golf Association took the bold decision to bring the 1929 US Amateur Championship to Pebble Beach, the first time a national championship was played west of the Mississippi. The event was a success, despite the plot being lost slightly when Bobby Jones, the great amateur then at the height of his extraordinary powers, was bundled out of the tournament in the first match-play round. Pebble Beach was now on the golfing map.

THE 7TH AT PEBBLE BEACH IS ONE OF THE MOST
CELEBRATED SHORT HOLES IN THE WORLD.

LOOKING ALONG THE 18TH AT PEBBLE BEACH
TOWARDS THE LODGE.

The US Amateur returned in 1947 and again in 1961 when the victor was Jack Nicklaus, the finest player of his generation. By then, however, the Del Monte Hotel had been purchased by the US Navy, and a large chunk of potential accommodation had been removed from the equation making it difficult for the USGA to bring its biggest tournament, the US Open, to Pebble Beach. Yet the public was clamouring to see how the finest golfers in the world would fare at Pebble Beach under US Open conditions — and the public knew all about the course, because from 1947 the Bing Crosby National Pro-Am golf tournament was hosted there. Television coverage (from 1958) and the presence of so many stars of stage, screen, and television soon made it a must-watch for millions. The tournament has mushroomed over the years, taking in three other neighbouring courses to become the AT&T Pebble Beach National Pro-Am, but the final round is still played at Pebble Beach and the long list of winners is about as good as it gets in professional golf.

Eventually the USGA took the risk, and in 1972 Pebble Beach hosted its first US Open. Jack Nicklaus demonstrated his continued liking for the course, winning by three shots. The script was good, the spectators turned up in droves, and the USGA brought its Open back ten years later.

Jack Nicklaus was again in the frame, except that this time he had the title whipped from under his nose by Tom Watson, who in a stroke of great fortune (not to mention brilliance) chipped in from a dreadful lie for a birdie-two on the 71st hole. After another ten-year gap the US Open came back, with Tom Kite triumphing in stormy conditions. Pebble Beach had revealed itself as a great championship course, so it came as no surprise when it was chosen to host the 100th US Open in 2000. On this occasion the young Tiger Woods demolished the rest of the field, winning by a record 15 strokes! The US Open returns to Pebble Beach in 2010.

PEBBLE BEACH'S 7TH GREEN, LOCATED ON THE ROCKS A FEW FEET ABOVE THE WAVES.

JACK NICKLAUS DESIGNED A NEW SHORT 5TH HOLE TO GIVE PABBLE BEACH AN EXTRA OCEANSIDE HOLE.

But Pebble Beach Resort is not simply one stunning golf course. For a start it has three supremely comfortable places to stay, each with its own distinctive style, and all offering superb service and a full range of amenities: The Lodge at Pebble Beach, Casa Palmero, and the Inn at Spanish Bay. There are thirteen different restaurants and bars serving food, and Pebble Beach Markets are richly stocked with fine food and over 800 wines, and will make up superb picnic baskets for the gourmet golfer.

Nor is Pebble Beach Golf Links the only course at the resort — far from it. The Del Monte Hotel may have long gone, but the Del Monte Golf Course still survives to this day and offers a truly delightful round on narrow, undulating fairways running through avenues of trees. Its greens are quite small and therefore present tricky targets.

Spyglass Hill is one of the toughest courses on the USPGA tour, and its 6th, 8th, and 16th holes are among the hardest the professionals face every year. It was designed by Robert Trent Jones and opened in 1966. Jones, the architect of hundreds of golf courses throughout the world in a long and prolific career, singled out Spyglass as one of his five favourites. It is not hard to see why. The first five holes run through sand dunes close to the shore, and the penalty for a missed fairway or green can be severe. Thereafter the course moves slightly inland, running through a forest of pines and cypresses, the narrowness of many fairways only adding to the difficulties posed by raised greens and occasional strategic water hazards. It is a great course, but one on which only the A-game will do.

The Links at Spanish Bay is almost certainly the last course to be built on this stretch of the California coastline, as complex conservation and planning issues will probably prevent any more. A joint project by Sandy Tatum, Tom Watson, and Robert Trent Jones Jr, the Links and Inn were opened in 1987. Their intention was to design and create a course in the spirit of the traditional old Scottish links with tumbling fairways and

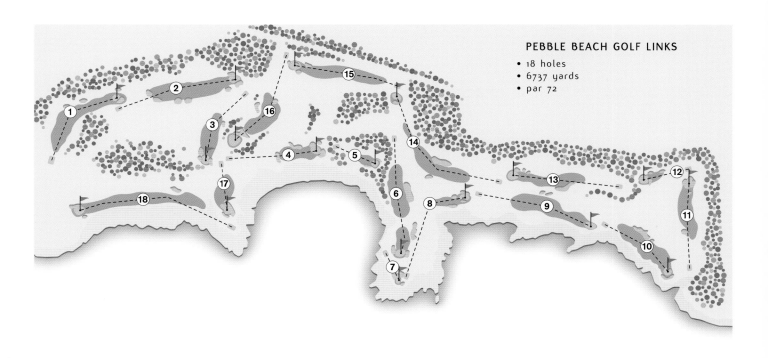

almost haphazard greens, very vulnerable to changes in the wind and demanding more of a ground game than an aerial one. This was an environmentally sensitive site, and the course had to be carefully routed to avoid disturbance to many indigenous plants and creatures. These parts of the course have been vigilantly preserved ever since. There is a charm and distinction to Spanish Bay which reflects Watson's love of British links golf. After all he was supremely good at playing it, winning five Open Championships between 1975 and 1983.

Like the USGA, the golfer seeking that something special will return to Pebble Beach. It is one of the very few US Open courses available for public play. And where can more exhilarating golf be found than in that magnificent stretch of ocean-side holes from the 4th to the 10th, which includes such gems as the diminutive 7th, played to a minuscule green surrounded by sand, rocks, and sea, and the 9th, the hardest of a trio of great cliff-top holes? Pebble Beach manages to save two more ocean-side holes for the finish, the testing par-3 17th and the great do-or-die 543-yard par-5 18th, where the hopes of so many potential tournament winners have foundered on the rocks along the shoreline. No wonder Jack Nicklaus has declared, "If I had only one more round to play, I would choose to play it at Pebble Beach."

Contact:

Pebble Beach Resorts
The Lodge at Pebble Beach
1700 17-Mile Drive
Pebble Beach
CA 93953
USA
Tel +1 (800) 654 9300
www.pebblebeach.com

Pinehurst, North Carolina, USA

The part of North Carolina known as the Carolina Sandhills is today a very desirable place to live. Its towns are small but classy, the climate gentle yet invigorating, and the pace of life such that people have the time to enquire of each other's health as a matter of southern courtesy. Towards the end of the 19th century the region was hardly known outside its own immediate neighbourhood, and it was during the 1890s that James Walker Tufts discovered it. He was a wealthy Bostonian who had made his money by building up a drug store empire, but he did not enjoy the best of health, especially during the bitter New England winters. It seemed to him that the Sandhills might offer him a better climate and a healthier lifestyle. During 1895 and 1896 he bought almost 5,000 hectares (13,000 acres) of timberland from a local family for a little over $15,000.

THE 15TH HOLE OF NO 4 COURSE, AN ORIGINAL DONALD ROSS DESIGN BUILT IN 1919 THAT WAS REDESIGNED BY TOM FAZIO IN 2000.

Tufts was a man who did things quickly and efficiently. He brought in a landscape architect Frederick Law Olmsted, who had designed New York's Central Park and Jackson Park in Chicago. Olmsted planned a small town, Pinehurst, centred on a village common with a church at one end and a town hall at the other. The Holly Inn opened on 31 December 1895, and Tufts advertised it among doctors in the northern states with the slogan, 'Consumptives welcome!' A year later it was discovered that tuberculosis was contagious, and his next advertisements bore the warning, 'Consumptives excluded!' Curiously, for many years thereafter a clause prohibiting the sale of houses at Pinehurst to those with tuberculosis was inserted into local property deeds.

A couple of years later, Tufts noticed that one or two of the Pinehurst residents had begun playing an embryonic form of golf on a few improvised holes. Tufts was himself a golfer, playing during the summer months at Oakley Country Club in Massachusetts. He recognized immediately the enormous potential for golf in the Sandhills. Dr. LeRoy Culver, an amateur designer, laid out the first nine holes, which were soon expanded to eighteen. In 1900 Harry Vardon, the great Jersey-born British golfer, arrived in Pinehurst to play several exhibition

rounds over the new course. In doing so he did much to raise the profile of Pinehurst golf. A few months later, in December 1900, the new professional at Oakley made the journey south to Pinehurst. He was Donald Ross.

Ross had grown up and learned his golf in Dornoch in the far north of Scotland. He had also spent some time learning the skills of a professional golfer from Old Tom Morris in St. Andrews. Later he returned to Dornoch to become the greenkeeper and professional. His pedigree was right for Tufts, Pinehurst, and the future of golf course design in the USA. First he set about redesigning the existing course, Pinehurst No. 1 More significantly he began the design and layout of Pinehurst No. 2.

On the face of it, the timberlands of inland North Carolina might seem to have little in common with Scottish links land, but in fact millions of years ago they lay beneath the sea and today the underlying soil is sand. Take the trees away and the ground is remarkably links-like. Ross had the good drainage he required, and there was plenty of water available for irrigation. He also had a detailed knowledge of the greatness and subtleties of the greens at St. Andrews, and especially Dornoch.

THE PAR-5 4TH OF NO. 2 COURSE, SET AMONG THE CAROLINA PINES.

Almost every green at Dornoch is raised above its surroundings, and the course is acknowledged as one of the great tests of the approach game. Ross set out to reproduce their challenge and succeeded brilliantly. Pinehurst No. 2, especially when prepared for a great championship, is a stringent test of all departments of the game, and because of the subtlety of the design it puts a great premium on the drive. Find the wrong part of the fairway and the following shot is next to impossible. Miss the fairway altogether

and serious trouble looms. Ross finished Pinehurst No. 2 in 1907, and added the third and fourth courses in 1910 and 1919, by which time he was established as the busiest and most prolific golf architect in the world. He had design offices in a number of parts of the USA, and greatly influenced the work of several succeeding generations of golf architects in North America. Not all Ross courses have survived, but those that do and are reasonably intact are highly prized by lovers of traditional golf.

Since the days of Ross four more courses have been added, No. 8 as recently as 1995. With so much golf available on one site, the Holly Inn could no longer accommodate so many visitors at one time under its modest roof. In 1901 the grand Carolina Hotel opened, and it has been the centrepiece of the Pinehurst Resort ever since. The Tufts family presided over the life and work of Pinehurst for many years, but it was sold in 1971. It seemed that the nature of Pinehurst would be changed for ever

by its new owners, but they in their turn sold the resort in 1984 to the Club Corporation of America, who happily have restored the uniquely relaxed yet formal ethos of Pinehurst.

Pinehurst is now an enormous operation. As well as the impressive Carolina (now a National Historic Landmark), it also boasts the Manor (seen as something of a sportsman's lodge), and the Holly Inn (which houses the 1895 Room, the resort's acclaimed and most prestigious restaurant). Nor is Pinehurst's expertise at growing grass confined to its golf courses: Pinehurst hosted the 2003 US Lawnbowls Championship, and it has croquet lawns, too. Its 24 clay tennis courts, meanwhile, are good enough to have hosted the 1994–6 US Clay Court Championships. The Beach Club overlooks the resort's 80-hectare (200-acre) freshwater lake, and in summer boats from kayaks to sailboats are available for hire. It goes without saying that fishing is also on offer, while the Spa will gently ease the aches and pains of the over-stretched sportsman or woman.

Tufts was not the only man to develop golf in the Pinehurst area: there are at least 25 other courses locally, many of them very good. Golf is not the only sporting development in the region, either. That sandy turf that characterizes the Sandhills is also ideal for a variety of equine pursuits. Since the close of the 19th century, horse-breeding, and training,

THE 18TH HOLE OF NO. 4 COURSE.

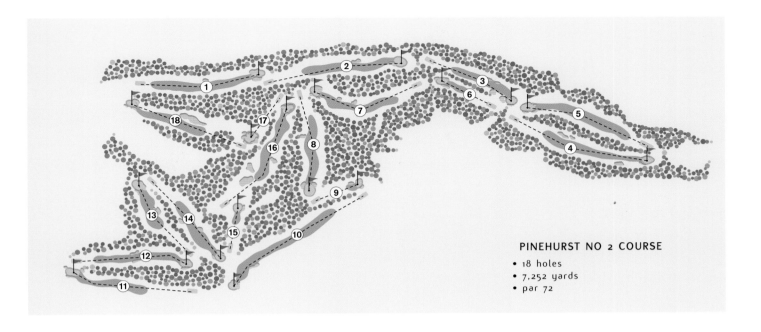

PINEHURST NO 2 COURSE
- 18 holes
- 7,252 yards
- par 72

racing on the flat and over fences, polo, trotting, eventing and showjumping have been a part of life here. Perhaps most prominent of all is foxhunting: the Moore County Hounds, founded in 1914 by James Boyd, are said to be the oldest private pack in the southern states.

In 1901, Pinehurst inaugurated the North and South Amateur Championship, and later it hosted the North and South Open Championship for professionals. It was at this tournament in 1940 that Ben Hogan won his first professional title. Four years before this, the USPGA Championship was held at Pinehurst, as were the 1951 Ryder Cup matches. Many amateur championships came to Pinehurst, such as the 1962 US Men's Amateur and 1989 US Women's Amateur, but it still lacked 'the big one'. Almost as if it were being

tried out for it, Pinehurst hosted the 1991 and 1992 US Tour Championships, the end of season decider for the final honours of that year's USPGA Tour, and then the US Senior US Open came in 1994. In 1999 'the big one' finally arrived, with Payne Stewart being a popular winner of that year's US Open. He had won because he was able to hold his nerve as the championship drew to a nail-biting conclusion, but he also took the trophy because he understood the exact nature of the test set by Ross, and how to adapt his game to hit and hold the treacherous greens. Pinehurst No. 2 course had shown that it could hold its head high, yielding nothing to the power and technique of today's golfing superstars. Almost immediately it was announced that the US Open would return there in 2005.

Contact:

Pinehurst Resort
1 Carolina Vista Drive
Village of Pinehurst
North Carolina 28374
USA
Tel: +1 910.235.8507
www.pinehurst.com

Address Book for all golfing resorts and clubs mentioned in the book:

Adare Manor Hotel and Golf Resort
Adare, Co. Limerick
Ireland
Tel: +353 (0)61 396566
Toll Free (USA and Canada): 1 800 462 3273
Freephone (UK): 0800 904 7523
Email: reservations@adaremanor.com
www.adaremanor.ie

The American Club
444 Highland Drive, Kohler
Wisconsin 53044
USA
Tel: +1 (800) 344 2838 Ext 700
Email via: www.destinationkohler.com

Ballybunion Golf Course
Ballybunion, Co. Kerry
Ireland
Tel: +353 (0)68 27146
Email: bbgolfc@iol.ie
www.ballybuniongolfclub.iel

Casa de Campo
PO Box 140, La Romana
Dominican Republic
Tel: +1-809 523 3333 or +1-809 523 8698
Email: reserva@ccampo.com.do
www.casadcampo.com

Crowne Plaza Liverpool
St. Nicholas Place, Princes Dock, Pier Head,
Liverpool L3 1QW
England
Tel: +44 (0)151 243 8000
Email: enquiries@cpliverpool.com
www.cpliverpool.com

The Empire Hotel and Country Club
The Empire Hotel & Country Club
Jerudong BG3122
Brunei Darussalam
Tel: +673 241 8888
Email: sales@theempirehotel.com
www.theempirehotel.com

Fairmont Banff Springs
405 Spray Avenue
Banff, Alberta
Canada T1L 1J4
Tel +1 (403) 762 2211
Email: banffsprings@fairmont.com
www.fairmont.com/banffsprings

Fairmont Jasper Park Lodge
Old Lodge Road
Jasper, Alberta
Canada T0E 1E0
Tel: +1 (780) 852 3301
Email: jasperparklodge@fairmont.com
www.fairmont.com/jasper

Fancourt Hotel and Country Club Estate
PO Box 2266, George
6530 South Africa
Tel: +27 (0)44 804 0000
Email: hotel@fancourt.co.za
www.fancourt.co.za

Fiesta Americana Grand
Tel: +52 624 145-6200
(from USA) 1 (800) FIESTA1
Fax: +52 624 145-6201
Email: reserv@fiestaamericana.com.mx

Four Seasons Resort Costa Rica
Peninsula de Papagayo, Guanacaste
Costa Rica
Tel: +506 696 0000
www.fourseasons.com/costarica/index.html

The Gleneagles Hotel
Auchterarder, Perthshire
Scotland PH3 1NF
Tel +44 (0)1764 662231
Email: resort.sales@gleneagles.com
www.gleneagles.com

The Greenbrier
300 W. Main Street
White Sulphur Springs
West Virginia 24988
Tel: +1 (800) 453 4858
Email via www.greenbrier.com

Heswall Golf Club
Cottage Lane, Heswall
Wirral CH60 8PB
England
Tel: +44(0) 151 342 1237
Email: dawn@heswallgolfclub.com
www.heswallgolfclub.com

Highlands Links
Cape Breton Highlands National Park
Ingonish Beach, Nova Scotia
Canada
Tel: 1-800-441-1118
Email: highlands.links@pc.gc.ca
www.highlandslinksgolf.com

Hope Island Resort
Hope Island Road
Hope Island, Queensland
Australia
Tel: +61 7 5530 9000
Email: via website www.hir.com.au/contact.asp
www.hir.com.au/home.asp

The Keltic Lodge
Middle Head Peninsula
Ingonish Beach, Nova Scotia
Canada B0C 1L0
Tel: +1 (902) 285 2880
(From USA) Toll Free: 1 800 565 0444
Email: keltic@signatureresorts.com
http://signatureresorts.com/index.asp

Lahinch Golf Club
Lahinch, Co. Clare
Ireland
Tel: +353 (0)65 7081003
Email: info@lahinchgolf.com
www.lahinchgolf.com

Les Bordes
41220 Saint-Laurent-Nouan
France
Tel: +33 (0) 450 26 85 00
Email: info@lesbordes.com
www.lesbordes.com

The Lodge at Kauri Cliffs
Matauri Bay Road, Matauri Bay
Northland
New Zealand
Tel: +64 9 407 0010
Email: info@kauricliffs.com
www.kauricliffs.com

Lodge at Koele
Lana'i Resort Reservations
PO Box 630310, Lana'i City
Hawai'i 96763
Tel: +1 (808) 450 3704
Email: reservations@lanai-resorts.com
www.lodgeatkoele.com

Manele Bay Hotel
Lana'i Resort Reservations
PO Box 630310, Lana'i City
Hawai'i 96763
Tel: +1 (808) 450 3704
Email: reservations@lanai-resorts.com
www.manelebayhotel.com

Old Course Hotel Golf Resort and Spa
St. Andrews, Fife, Scotland KY16 9SP
Tel: +44 (0)1334 474371
http://oldcoursehotel.co.uk

Pebble Beach Resort
The Lodge at Pebble Beach
1700 17-Mile Drive, Pebble Beach
CA 93953
USA
Tel +1 (800) 654 9300
www.pebblebeach.com

Pinehurst Resort
1 Carolina Vista Drive
Village of Pinehurst
North Carolina 28374
USA
Tel: +1 910.235.8507
www.pinehurst.com

Quinta do Lago
Almancil, Algarve
8135-024 Portugal
Tel: +351 289 350 350
Email: info@quintadolagohotel.com
www.hotelquintadolago.com

Royal Liverpool Golf Club
Meols Drive, Hoylake, Wirral CH47 4AL
England
Tel: +44 (0)151 632 3101
Email: sec@royal-liverpool-golf.com
www.royal-liverpool-golf.com

Royal Parc Evian
74500 Evian-les-Bains
France
Tel: +33 (0)450 26 85 00
Email: reservation@royalparcevian.com
www.royalparcevian.com

St. Andrews Bay Resort and Spa
Tel: +44 (0)1334 837000
Email: info@standrewsbay.com
www.standrewsbay.com

St. Andrews Links Trust
Pilmour House, St. Andrews, Fife
Scotland KY16 9SF
Tel: +44 (0)1334 466666
Email: enquiries@standrews.org.uk

The San Roque Club
C.N. 340 KM 127
11360 San Roque (Cádiz)
Spain
Tel: +34 956 613 030
Email: info@sanroqueclub.com
www.sanroqueclub.com

Sheraton Hacienda del Mar
Tel: +52 624 145 8000
(from USA) 1 (888) 672 7137
Fax: +52 624 145 8002
Email:
information@sheratonhaciendadelmar.com

Stoke Park Club
Park Road, Stoke Poges, Bucks
England, SL2 4PG
Tel: +44 (0)1753 717171
Email: info@stokeparkclub.com
www.stokeparkclub.com/index.php

Sunningdale Golf Club
Ridgemount Road
Sunningdale, Berkshire
England, SL5 9RR
Tel: +44 (0)1344 621681
www.sunningdale-golfclub.co.uk

Wallsey Golf Club
Bayswater Road, Wallsey
Wirral CH45 8LA
England
Tel: +44(0) 151 691 1024
Email: info@wallaseygolfclub.com
www.wallaseygolfclub.com

Waterville Golf Links
Waterville, Co. Kerry
Ireland
Tel: +353 (0)66 9474102
Email: wvgolf@iol.ie
www.watervillegolflinks.ie

The Wentworth Club
Wentworth Drive,
Virginia Water, Surrey
England, GU25 4LS
Tel: +44 (0)1344 842201
www.wentworthgolf.co.uk

Westin Turnberry Resort
Turnberry, Ayrshire
Scotland
KA26 9LT
Tel: +44 (0)1655 331000
Email: turnberry@westin.com
www.turnberry.co.uk

Picture credits

The publisher would like to thank the following photographers, agencies, golf resorts and clubs for their kind permission to reproduce the photographs in this book:

4 © Kauri Cliffs Lodge and Golf Course; 6 Tony Roberts/Corbis; 8–12 Courtesy of the Hope Island Resort Golf Club; 14–18 © The Empire Hotel and Country Club, Brunei; 20–23 Courtesy of the Fairmont Banff Springs; 24 © Evan Schiller; 26–30 Courtesy of the Fairmont Jasper Park; 32–36 Nova Scotia Tourism, Culture and Heritage; 38 © Four Seasons Resort Costa Rica; 40–41 © John and Jeannine Henebry; 42 © Four Seasons Resort Costa Rica; 44 Casa de Campo, La Romana, DR; 46 Tony Roberts/Corbis; 47–48 Casa de Campo, La Romana, DR; 50 Eric Hepworth; 52–53 Phil Sheldon Golf Picture Library; 54 © Reuters/Corbis; 56 © Stoke Park Club; 58 Hobbs Golf Collection; 59 Tony Roberts/Corbis; 62 Phil Sheldon Golf Picture Library; 64–66 © Les Bordes Resort; 68–72 J.N.Reichel/ Royal Parc Evian; 74–77 © Evan Schiller; 78 Patrick Drickey/Stonehouse Publishing Co.; 80–84 John and Jeannine Henebry; 86–90 © Kauri Cliffs Lodge and Golf Course; 92–95 Courtesy of Hotel Quinta da Lago; 96 Phil Sheldon Golf Picture Library; 98 © The Gleneagles Hotel; 99 Hobbs Golf Collection; 100–102 © The Gleneagles Hotel; 104 Gary Doak/Scottish Viewpoint Picture Library; 105 Hobbs Golf Collection; 106–108 Phil Sheldon Golf Picture Library; 110 Matthew Harris/The Golf Picture Library; 113–114 Phil Sheldon Golf Picture Library; 116–120 © Fancourt Hotel and Country Club Estate; 122 Phil Sheldon Golf Picture Library; 124 Anton Meres/Reuters/Corbis; 125 Phil Sheldon Golf Picture Library; 126 Marcelo del Poso/Reuters/Corbis; 128 Courtesy of The American Club, Kohler/Kohler Co.; 130–131 Patrick Drickey/Stonehouse Publishing Co.; 132 Courtesy The American Club Kohler/Kohler Co.; 134 Courtesy of The Greenbrier; 136 Phil Sheldon Golf Picture Library; 137–138 © Evan Schiller; 140–144 Courtesy of the Island of Lana'i; 146 Larry Lambrecht/Lambrecht Photography; 148 © 2004 Joann Dost/Reproduced by permission of Pebble Beach Company; 150 Patrick Drickey/Stonehouse Publishing Co.; 152 © Pinehurst, Inc.; 154–155 Patrick Drickey/ Stonehouse Publishing Co.; 156 © Pinehurst, Inc.

Every effort has been made to trace the images' copyright holders. We apologise in advance for any unintentional omissions, and would be pleased to insert the appropriate acknowledgment in any subsequent printing.

More Exceptional Destinations from Abbeville Press:

Cooking School Holidays
In the World's Most Exceptional Places

JENNI MUIR

150 full-color illustrations
160 pages • 8¼ X 9½"
Cloth • ISBN 0-7892-0836-9 • $29.95

Woodstock Inn & Resort

Spas
Exceptional Destinations Around the World

ELOISE NAPIER

240 full-color illustrations
160 pages • 8¼ X 9½"
Cloth • ISBN 0-7892-0798-2 • $29.95

Chiva Som

Bicycling
Along the World's Most Exceptional Routes

ROB PENN

100 full-color illustrations
160 pages • 8¼ X 9½"
Cloth • ISBN 0-7892-0846-6 • $29.95

Glenn Rowley/KE Adventure Travel

Walking
The World's Most Exceptional Trails

ELOISE NAPIER

240 full-color illustrations
160 pages • 8¼ X 9½"
Cloth • ISBN: 0-7892-0801-6 • $29.95

Courtesy of ATG Oxford